INCREDIBLE HISTORY
WONDERS
OF THE WORLD

INCREDIBLE HISTORY
WONDERS
OF THE WORLD

DK

DK Penguin Random House

Senior Editors Sam Kennedy, Anna Streiffert Limerick
Senior Art Editor Stefan Podhorodecki
Editorial team Ian Fitzgerald, Camilla Hallinan, Justine Willis
Design team Mik Gates, Beth Johnston
3-D illustrators Art Agency: Barry Croucher, Jean-Michel Girard;
ArtistPartners: Angelo Rinaldi, Paul Young;
Chris@KJA Artists; Peter Bull Art Studio; Sofian Moumene
Picture Researcher Sarah Hopper
Creative Retouching Stefan Podhorodecki
Managing Editor Francesca Baines
Managing Art Editor Philip Letsu
Production Editor Jacqueline Street-Elkayam
Senior Production Controller Poppy David
Jacket Designer Akiko Kato
Senior Jackets Coordinator Priyanka Sharma-Saddi
Jacket Design Development Manager Sophia MTT
Publisher Andrew Macintyre
Art Director Karen Self
Associate Publishing Director Liz Wheeler
Publishing Director Jonathan Metcalf

Contributors Ian Fitzgerald, Lizzie Munsey

Specialist Consultants
Dr Crispin Branfoot; Professor Shadreck Chirikure;
Professor Paul Collins PhD; Professor Joann Fletcher; Professor
Elizabeth Graham; Dr Susan Greaney; Henry Hurst; Dr Anders
Karlsson; Professor Elizabeth James; Professor Colin Jones;
Stephen Kay, FSA; William Lindesay, OBE; Professor Hannah
Mattson; Dr Anna McSweeney; Dr John Miksic; David Stuttard;
Dr Marlena Whiting; Professor Peter Wilson

First published in Great Britain in 2023
Dorling Kindersley Limited
DK, One Embassy Gardens, 8 Viaduct Gardens,
London, SW11 7BW

The authorised representative in the EEA is
Dorling Kindersley Verlag GmbH. Arnulfstr. 124,
80636 Munich, Germany

Copyright © 2023 Dorling Kindersley Limited
A Penguin Random House Company
10 9 8 7 6 5 4 3 2 1
001–333631–April/2023

A CIP catalogue record for this book is available
from the British Library.
ISBN: 978-0-2415-9573-2

Printed and bound in the UAE

For the curious
www.dk.com

MIX
Paper | Supporting
responsible forestry
FSC™ C018179

This book was made with Forest Stewardship Council™
certified paper – one small step in DK's commitment to a
sustainable future. For more information go to
www.dk.com/our-green-pledge

CONTENTS

06 THE SEVEN WONDERS
OF THE ANCIENT WORLD

08 TIME TRAVEL

10 STONEHENGE, ENGLAND, UK

20 ISHTAR GATE, IRAQ

26 MALQATA, EGYPT

34 HARBOUR OF CARTHAGE,
TUNISIA

42 PETRA, JORDAN

48 ACROPOLIS, GREECE

58	COLOSSEUM, ITALY
70	SIGIRIYA, SRI LANKA
76	CHICHEN ITZA, MEXICO
86	HAGIA SOPHIA, TURKEY
96	BOROBUDUR, INDONESIA
102	PUEBLO BONITO, NEW MEXICO, USA
108	ALHAMBRA, SPAIN
114	GREAT ZIMBABWE, ZIMBABWE

120	HEIDELBERG CASTLE, GERMANY
126	DOSAN SEOWON, SOUTH KOREA
132	VERSAILLES, FRANCE
144	FORBIDDEN CITY, CHINA

156	GLOSSARY
158	INDEX
160	ACKNOWLEDGEMENTS

1. Statue of Zeus

Housed in its temple at Olympia, Greece, this 12-m (39-ft) high ivory and gold figure of the Greek god Zeus was worshipped by visitors to the ancient Olympic Games. It was created in 430 BCE by Phidias, the greatest sculptor of his time.

THE SEVEN WONDERS OF THE ANCIENT WORLD

Throughout history, people across the world have built many spectacular structures. This book tells the stories of 18 of these architectural wonders, set on five continents. The map on these pages, however, shows the ones often called the "Seven Wonders of the World" – they are seven buildings and monuments that amazed the people who lived around the Mediterranean in ancient times. All except one of these are gone now – do you know which one?

3. Mausoleum at Halicarnassus

This massive tomb from c. 350 BCE was named for Mausolus, the man who was buried here. Built in what is now Turkey (Türkiye), it was destroyed by earthquakes between the 12th and 15th centuries.

2. Temple of Artemis

Twice the size of the famous Parthenon in Athens, this was the greatest and largest temple in the ancient Mediterranean. It stood in Ephesus, in modern-day Turkey (Türkiye), and was built for the Greek goddess of the hunt.

4. Colossus of Rhodes

This giant effigy of the Greek sun god, Helios, was built to stand across Rhodes' harbour entrance in 280 BCE, to mark the island's victory in war over Macedonia. The ancient world's biggest statue, it collapsed during an earthquake in 226 BCE.

7. Hanging Gardens of Babylon

According to legend, Queen Amytis of Babylon (now Iraq) missed the green hills of her native Media (Iran) so much that her husband, King Nebuchadnezzar II, built huge gardens for her in around 605 BCE.

6. Great Pyramid of Giza

The oldest of these ancient wonders is the only one that still exists today. It was made for the Egyptian pharaoh Khufu around 2560 BCE. Nearly 140 m (460 ft) high, it was the world's tallest building for almost 4,500 years.

5. Lighthouse of Alexandria

A massive beacon, 100 m (330 ft) high, it guided ships sailing into the city's harbour on the Nile Delta from the 3rd century BCE until its collapse in the 1300s. By day, its light signal came from a mirror reflecting sunlight. At night, a fire was the light source.

MEDITERRANEAN SEA

1 2 3 4 5 6 7

TIME TRAVEL

From the ancient palace of a pharaoh at Malqata, Egypt, to the thousand-year-old multi-storey housing of the people of Pueblo Bonito in the USA, the world is full of ruins of once splendid buildings. This book brings these wonders back to life, and tells the incredible histories of the people who built them.

4. Stonehenge

Was it a Stone Age temple, or astronomical structure? What did the people who once gathered here do? At more than 5,000 years old, this gigantic stone circle is one of Britain's most ancient and mysterious monuments.

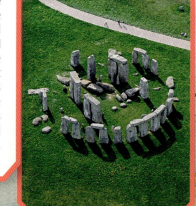

1. Pueblo Bonito

At the foot of a steep cliff in New Mexico, USA, this was the largest settlement of the Pueblo people in Chaco Canyon. Constructed from the 9th century onwards, it was abandoned some 400 years later.

2. Chichen Itza

Dominated by the great step pyramid of Kukulcan, the city of Chichen Itza in Mexico was built by the Maya who once ruled this region. Other buildings reveal their keen interest in astronomy and ballgames.

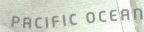

3. Great Zimbabwe

Spread out across a large area in what is now Zimbabwe, this site was a busy trading centre in the 9th–16th centuries. It was home to royal rulers, farmers, artisans, and merchants. Its remaining towers and mighty walls only hint at its former glory.

ARCTIC OCEAN

ATLANTIC OCEAN

PACIFIC OCEAN

5. Colosseum
Opened in 80 CE so that the Romans could watch gladiator fights and beast hunts, Rome's ancient arena is an architectural and engineering masterpiece that, even half-ruined, still takes the breath away.

9. Dosan Seowon
In the 16th century, this academy in South Korea was full of young students learning about Confucian philosophy. Today, it is a shrine and museum.

VERSAILLES
France

HAGIA SOPHIA
Turkey

HEIDELBERG
Germany

ACROPOLIS
Greece

ISHTAR GATE
Iraq

MALQATA
Egypt

FORBIDDEN CITY
China

HARBOUR OF CARTHAGE
Tunisia

ALHAMBRA
Spain

ATLANTIC OCEAN

INDIAN OCEAN

7. Sigiriya
Perched 180 m (590 ft) up on a column of rock, Sigiriya in central Sri Lanka was both a fortress and a palace in the 5th century. At its foot are some of the oldest landscaped gardens in the world.

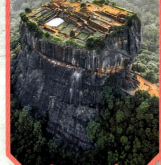

6. Petra
Ancient travellers in the deserts of Jordan were amazed when entering Petra, an entire city carved into pink sandstone cliffs. The buildings of the 2,000-year-old city still astonish visitors today.

8. Borobudur
This huge shrine to the Buddha rises above the forests of Java, one of the islands in Indonesia. Built in the 9th century, it is now an important site of pilgrimage for Buddhists worldwide.

STONE CIRCLE

The colossal monoliths (standing stones) of Stonehenge, UK, have been a landmark for thousands of years. The earliest features, a circular ditch and a pair of earthen banks either side of it, were made about 5,000 years ago. The first stone circle was built in around 2,500 BCE, then more standing stones, pits, and earthworks were added over time. It is not known why it was built, but the position of the stones suggests it had something to do with the Sun and seasons.

North Sea

UK

Stonehenge

Southern monolith
Stonehenge is located on Salisbury Plain, in the south of the UK. The stones are surrounded by open countryside and farmland. There are several Neolithic (late Stone Age) sites nearby, but their exact link to Stonehenge is unknown.

Circles of stones
There are two types of stones at Stonehenge: sarsens and bluestones. The larger sarsens form the outer circle and a horseshoe shape inside it. The smaller bluestones were originally set up in two arcs, but were rearranged around 300 years later, to form an outer circle and inner oval.

This photographer has climbed a makeshift tower to photograph the stones' original joints.

 1 The circular ditch around Stonehenge was dug in around 3,000 BCE.

Rebuilding Stonehenge
By the 20th century, many of Stonehenge's stones had fallen over and lay on the ground. In the 1950s, archaeologists decided to restore some of the stones to make the monument easier to understand. Several were lifted back up into place.

The main entrance to the stone circle lines up with the Heel Stone.

Mysterious markings
Curious finds in the area around Stonehenge point to it being a site of importance. This chalk tablet was buried in a pit 2 km (1.2 miles) from Stonehenge, around 4,700 years ago. Its meaning, or why it was buried, is not known.

Intricate line patterns cover the tablet.

The Heel Stone
Outside the stone circle stands the large, lonely Heel Stone. Its position marks the point where the Sun rises on the summer solstice (the longest day of the year), when the sunrise is viewed from the centre of the circle.

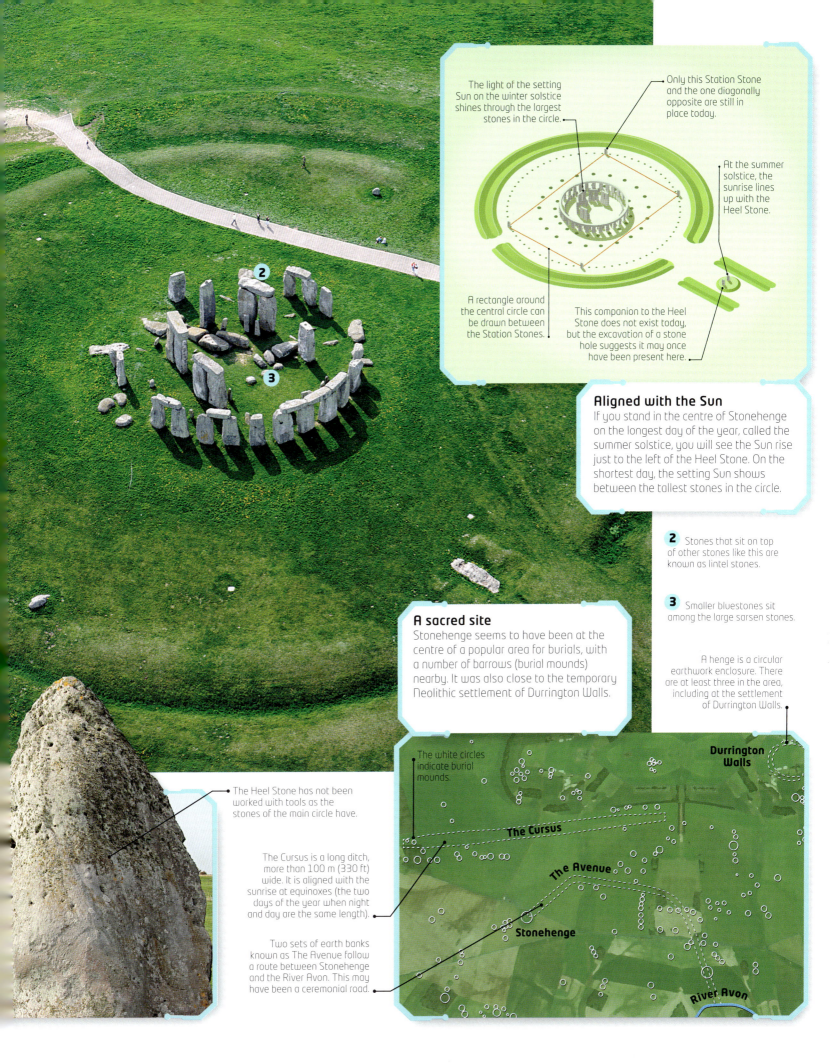

The light of the setting Sun on the winter solstice shines through the largest stones in the circle.

Only this Station Stone and the one diagonally opposite are still in place today.

At the summer solstice, the sunrise lines up with the Heel Stone.

A rectangle around the central circle can be drawn between the Station Stones.

This companion to the Heel Stone does not exist today, but the excavation of a stone hole suggests it may once have been present here.

Aligned with the Sun

If you stand in the centre of Stonehenge on the longest day of the year, called the summer solstice, you will see the Sun rise just to the left of the Heel Stone. On the shortest day, the setting Sun shows between the tallest stones in the circle.

2 Stones that sit on top of other stones like this are known as lintel stones.

3 Smaller bluestones sit among the large sarsen stones.

A henge is a circular earthwork enclosure. There are at least three in the area, including at the settlement of Durrington Walls.

A sacred site

Stonehenge seems to have been at the centre of a popular area for burials, with a number of barrows (burial mounds) nearby. It was also close to the temporary Neolithic settlement of Durrington Walls.

The Heel Stone has not been worked with tools as the stones of the main circle have.

The Cursus is a long ditch, more than 100 m (330 ft) wide. It is aligned with the sunrise at equinoxes (the two days of the year when night and day are the same length).

Two sets of earth banks known as The Avenue follow a route between Stonehenge and the River Avon. This may have been a ceremonial road.

The white circles indicate burial mounds.

Durrington Walls

The Cursus

The Avenue

Stonehenge

River Avon

MIDWINTER SUNSET

It is the winter solstice – the shortest day of the year. The longest night will soon begin. As the Sun sets, its light dips down between the two tallest stones at the bend of Stonehenge's inner horseshoe. People have gathered together here to celebrate that the days will now start to become longer. At the very centre of the circle stands a holy man, his arms raised as he conducts a ceremony.

1 Sarsen stones
Stonehenge's main structure is built from around 80 of these huge sarsen stones.

2 Bluestone circle
The smaller bluestones stand inside the outer ring. They are not joined to other stones.

3 Tongue and groove
The lintel stones have been carefully carved so that they can fit closely together.

4 Standing stones
The setting Sun shines through these sarsen stones at the centre of the ring.

5 On guard
Keepers make sure that only those permitted enter into the stone circle.

6 The Altar Stone
The Sun's rays spill onto this stone, which is of different rock from the sarsen and bluestones.

7 Leading the ceremony
Everyone's attention is on the holy man. He chants the midwinter ritual for all to hear.

8 New arrangement
A man is admiring the new position of these bluestones that used to stand elswehere.

9 Station Stones
Four outlying stones mark the corners of a square beyond the central circle of Stonehenge.

10 Looking in
Travellers are keen to catch a glimpse of the important happenings inside the circle.

11 All wrapped up
It is freezing cold at midwinter. People are wrapped up in warm layers of fur and leather.

The horizontal lintel stones are carefully placed using wooden platforms.

RAISING THE STONES

One of the sarsen stones has been cut into shape and is ready to be raised into place. It was brought to the site on timber rollers, and a pit has been dug where it will stand. Now, the last few preparations have been made, and the hard, heavy work of lifting the stone into its final position has only just begun when one of the ropes snaps, sending the stone crashing down!

Lumps called tenons have been carved into the tops of the stones. The lintels have matching holes for them to slot into.

A wooden structure has been built around the stone, with ropes securing it. A heavy weight attached to the bottom of the stone helps to tip it into an upright position.

The stone has been lowered into a deep hole with one sloped side, which the stone is currently leaning against. Once the stone is raised, the hole will be packed with rubble, to keep the stone upright.

As the people pull, the ropes will tighten, and eventually lift the stone upright. A wooden A-frame is used to help spread the stone's weight.

Brought across Britain

Stonehenge's smaller bluestones came from the Preseli Hills in Wales, UK, 290 km (180 miles) from the site. It is unclear whether these stones were floated on rafts or dragged over land. The larger sarsen stones came from the Marlborough Downs, 32 km (20 miles) from Stonehenge.

Preseli Hills
WALES
North Sea
UK
Alternative overland route
Marlborough Downs
Probable route by raft
Bristol Channel
Stonehenge

0 25mi
0 50km

Bluestone route
Sarsen stone route
ENGLAND

Each **sarsen stone** weighs around **25.4 tonnes (28 tons),** the same as **four African elephants.**

HAMMERSTONES

Construction tools

The builders of Stonehenge used a range of tools. The colossal rocks were shaped using different-sized hammerstones. Picks made from antlers were used for digging ditches and moving earth.

Large rocks were used to shape the boulders of Stonehenge. People then used smaller rocks to refine the shape.

ANTLER PICK

The source of the stones

Analysis shows Stonehenge's bluestones were quarried at sites in the Preseli Hills, Wales, UK. Some of them were placed in a circle at the end of The Avenue (see page 11) before being moved to Stonehenge.

A huge amount of strength is needed to lift the stone. Two rows of men and women have lined up to heave.

Neolilthic men probably had beards and long hair.

People of the past

Humans lived at Stonehenge long before the henge was built. This reconstruction is based on a 5,500-year-old skull of a man, found a short distance from the site. It shows how one of the local people may have looked.

VILLAGE LIFE

Just 3.2 km (2 miles) north of Stonehenge is the bustling settlement of Durrington Walls. This is where the henge's builders sleep, work, and celebrate. It is a temporary village, occupied only during festival times, when people flock here from all over Britain. People have brought their animals with them, ready for the season's feasts.

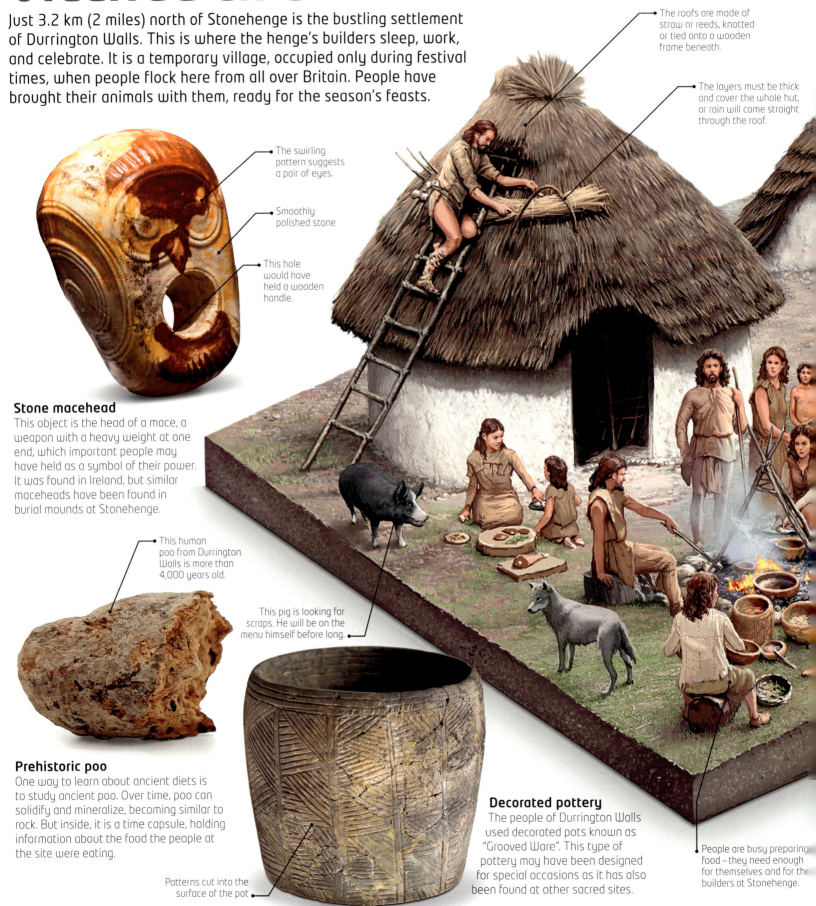

The roofs are made of straw or reeds, knotted or tied onto a wooden frame beneath.

The layers must be thick and cover the whole hut, or rain will come straight through the roof.

The swirling pattern suggests a pair of eyes.

Smoothly polished stone

This hole would have held a wooden handle.

Stone macehead
This object is the head of a mace, a weapon with a heavy weight at one end, which important people may have held as a symbol of their power. It was found in Ireland, but similar maceheads have been found in burial mounds at Stonehenge.

This human poo from Durrington Walls is more than 4,000 years old.

This pig is looking for scraps. He will be on the menu himself before long.

Prehistoric poo
One way to learn about ancient diets is to study ancient poo. Over time, poo can solidify and mineralize, becoming similar to rock. But inside, it is a time capsule, holding information about the food the people at the site were eating.

Patterns cut into the surface of the pot

Decorated pottery
The people of Durrington Walls used decorated pots known as "Grooved Ware". This type of pottery may have been designed for special occasions as it has also been found at other sacred sites.

People are busy preparing food – they need enough for themselves and for the builders at Stonehenge.

Each hut has a single hearth in its centre, and no windows. The air inside is thick with smoke.

Pigs were popular, as they have big litters of young and grow quickly. Rotten patches on pigs' teeth found at the site suggest they might have been given sweet foods at some point before they were killed, to make their meat even tastier.

Visitors have travelled here from across Britain. They are meeting up with people they have not seen all year.

Meat for the feast

The people who built Stonehenge were expert farmers, raising animals for meat and milk. Huge numbers of animal bones have been found at Durrington Walls. Some belonged to cows, but most were from pigs. Analysis of the bones shows that some of these animals were brought from as far away as Wales and northern England.

Reconstructed huts

Archaeologists have built a number of huts at Stonehenge using the materials and methods of the original builders. The walls are made of wattle and daub – clay and dung plastered over panels of woven branches.

Fences are made of wattle – sticks woven horizontally across upright posts.

The gold has tiny, evenly spaced marks.

Bones from recent feasts litter the ground around the settlement.

Golden hairclip

Many burial mounds have been found near Stonehenge. As well as bodies, they contain some surprisingly precious goods. This golden hair clip is one of two that were found with the body of the so-called "Amesbury Archer", who must have been a very wealthy man.

WEATHERED STONES
Today, the stones at Stonehenge look grey and mossy, even in the light of the rising sun. When they were freshly cut, however, the two rock types used would each have had their own colour – the sarsen stones would be whitish, while the bluestones looked dark blue.

BABYLONIAN GATE

Located in present-day Iraq, Babylon was once capital of a great empire, and the Ishtar Gate was a fittingly grand entrance leading to its main palace and temple quarter. Here, the royal family lived in luxury and the priests performed their religious rites to Ishtar, the goddess to whom the gate was dedicated. Close to the gate, at least in legend, were the famous Hanging Gardens of Babylon (see page 7). The gate is one of several Babylonian buildings to have been uncovered by archaeologists.

Birthplace of civilization
Babylon, in modern Iraq, lies beside the Euphrates River, which with the Tigris River formed "Mesopotamia", the area where the world's first cities were built.

Layer upon layer
The Ishtar Gate was excavated by German archaeologists over a period of 12 years from 1902. Excavations revealed that brick layers had been added on top of older layers, buried over time. Controversially, many of the colourful glazed bricks adorning the upper layers were taken back to Germany. What is left on the site are the oldest, unglazed layers of the structure.

1 These, the most ancient parts of the gate, got buried by soil and debris. The king built the famous blue glazed gate on top of them.

2 Concrete covers protect this passage on the Processional Way from being damaged by people walking over the ancient ruins.

3 The walls and towers along the Processional Way were once decorated with glazed lions, symbols of the goddess Ishtar.

The rod and ring symbolize the authority given by the gods to kings, as well as this goddess's power.

The dragon of Marduk, the supreme god of Babylon, lies beside an altar topped with Marduk's symbol.

Although it is not known for sure, these images may represent constellations. The horse in the archway could be a group of stars known as the Rainbow.

The bull figure, which also appears on the Ishtar Gate, represents the storm god Adad. The bull has a forked lightning bolt on its back.

Ruler of the night
The Babylonians had many gods and goddesses. This clay figure probably represents Ishtar's sister Ereshkigal, the queen of the underworld. The lions at her clawed feet represent her strength; the owls show that she ruled the night.

The writing is called cuneiform. It was made by pressing the end of a sharpened reed into damp clay to leave wedge shapes.

Boundary marker
This stele, or free-standing monument, is a legal document. The carved symbols of the gods were thought to protect the agreement. On the back and sides, it records a grant of land from King Nebuchadnezzar I, dating from around 1100 BCE.

Babylonian map of the world
Dating from the era of Nebuchadnezzar II, the builder of the Ishtar Gate, this clay map of the world shows Babylon in the middle. The circle on the outside is the "Bitter River" – the limits of the world of people, beyond which were the mythical lands.

The Babylonian language, written in cuneiform script, is part of the same family as Arabic and Hebrew.

Building certificate
Nebuchadnezzar II (r. 605–562 BCE) had this clay cylinder made to mark his strengthening of the city walls. It reads, in part: "I built a strong wall that cannot be shaken with bitumen and baked bricks... I laid its foundation on the breast of the netherworld, and I built its top as high as a mountain."

1 Special street
The Processional Way is paved in stone and bricks, unlike most other roads in the city.

2 Giving praise
Merchants and their customers wave, cheer, and chant as the holy procession passes by.

3 Main god
Marduk, also known as Bel (or "lord"), travels behind Adad. Behind him comes Ishtar.

4 Holy men
The high priest of Marduk and other religious officials walk alongside their god.

5 Come inside
The outer gate's huge cedar wood and bronze doors will open to allow the procession to enter.

6 Top temple
The temple at the top of the Etemenanki ziggurat was used as a place of worship.

PARADE OF GODS

Babylon's market traders and shoppers look on in wonder as the city's priests pass along the Processional Way towards the Ishtar Gate. They accompany a newly-made effigy of Babylon's chief god, Marduk, as well as images of other deities such as Adad, the god of storms, and Ishtar herself, goddess of love, justice, and war. The sacred statues are transported to their shrines where the people will come to pray and worship.

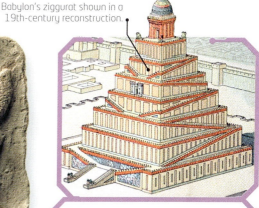

Babylon's ziggurat shown in a 19th-century reconstruction.

Symbolic beast
Known as a Mushkhushshu, this mythological dragon was the sacred animal of the chief god, Marduk. It appears many times on the Ishtar Gate, as well as on smaller objects throughout Babylon, such as on this clay plaque.

Stepped tower
All Babylonian cities had a ziggurat, a stepped tower with a temple at the summit. Babylon's ziggurat was called Etemenanki, which means "the temple platform linking heaven and Earth".

Terrific tiles
The gate is made of baked mud bricks, most of which were coated in a glass-like deep blue glaze. The animals were created with bricks individually moulded to form the body shape and then glazed a different colour.

Cuneiform script
Most Babylonian cuneiform (wedge-shaped) inscriptions were made in clay, but this is a rare example where it is carved in stone. It records the building works of Nebuchadnezzar in the city of Babylon.

7 **Inner gate**
This fortified gateway is 15.2 m (50 ft) high. Its mud bricks are held together with tar.

8 **Keeping guard**
An armed soldier wearing his bronze helmet, or *huliam*, looks out for trouble.

A PALACE IN RUINS

In the heart of Egypt, not far from the River Nile, lie crumbled ruins that were once the magnificent palace complex of Malqata. Part of a festival city, it was built by Pharaoh Amenhotep III in the 14th century BCE for his Heb Sed (jubilee) celebrations. Malqata was linked to the Nile by canals, so the pharaoh could travel anywhere without his feet touching land.

Place of celebrations
The palace of Malqata was located in Upper Egypt, on the west bank of the Nile, opposite the great city of Thebes, and the temple of Luxor.

Pleasing the gods
The ancient Egyptians worshipped hundreds of gods, who each had their own role. The gods Aten, Amun, Horus, and Hathor were all associated with the jubilee festivals celebrated at Malqata.

This wall painting from the tomb of Amenhotep III shows him with a number of gods and goddesses.

Glorious glass
Egypt under Amenhotep III was very wealthy, and riches were spent on luxury items. Egyptian artisans began to produce fine glass vases and other vessels. Many have been found in the tombs of the Egyptian elite.

This is a modern reconstruction of a cartouche of Amenhotep III that was found at Malqata.

Royal seal
The names of pharaohs were always written inside an oval shape, called a cartouche. Malqata was decorated with blue-and-gold cartouches, carved with the official throne name of Amenhotep III.

Amenhotep the Magnificent
Amenhotep III was Egypt's richest pharaoh, and ruled from 1386 to 1353 BCE. Known as the Sun King, Amenhotep III oversaw a golden age. He launched many grand building projects and rarely needed to go to war.

In this sculpture, Amenhotep III (right) stands next to Sobek the crocodile god (left).

This section of a palace painting features the heads of bulls.

House of the arts
Rooms were filled with colourful furniture, pottery, glassware, and ceiling and wall paintings. These paintings featured animals, gods and goddesses, patterns, and the pharaoh's name. Many painting fragments now lie on the ground.

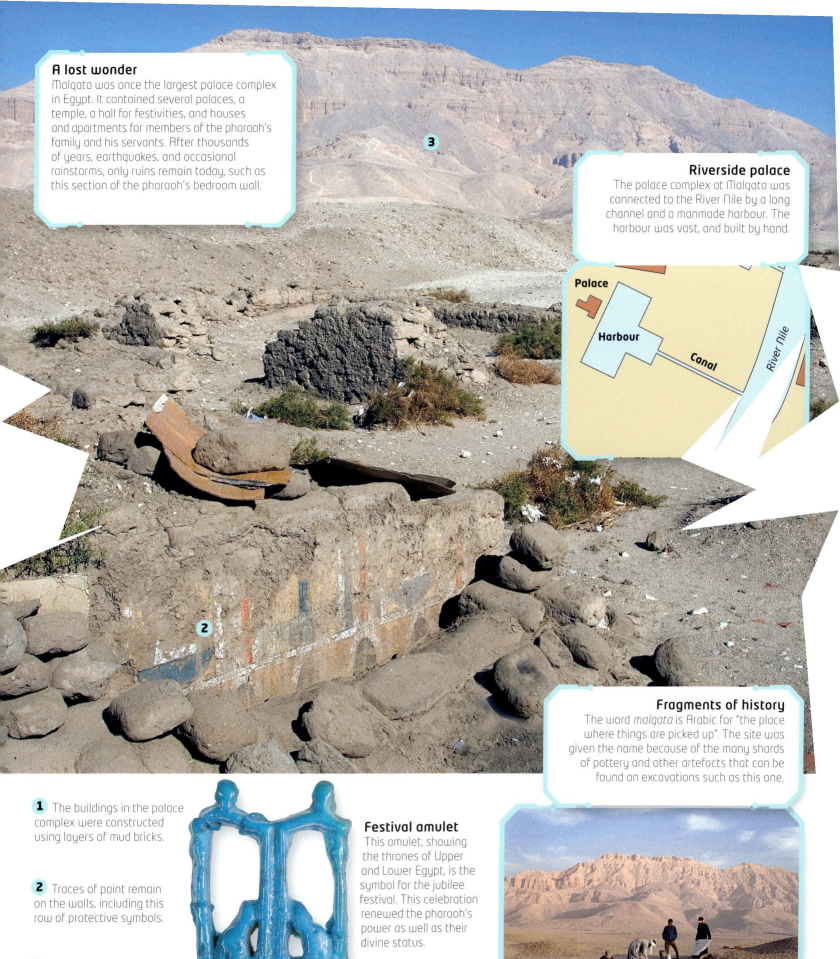

A lost wonder
Malqata was once the largest palace complex in Egypt. It contained several palaces, a temple, a hall for festivities, and houses and apartments for members of the pharaoh's family and his servants. After thousands of years, earthquakes, and occasional rainstorms, only ruins remain today, such as this section of the pharaoh's bedroom wall.

Riverside palace
The palace complex at Malqata was connected to the River Nile by a long channel and a manmade harbour. The harbour was vast, and built by hand.

Palace

Harbour

Canal

River Nile

Fragments of history
The word *malqata* is Arabic for "the place where things are picked up". The site was given the name because of the many shards of pottery and other artefacts that can be found on excavations such as this one.

1 The buildings in the palace complex were constructed using layers of mud bricks.

2 Traces of paint remain on the walls, including this row of protective symbols.

3 Limestone cliffs rise up behind the remains of the palace complex.

Festival amulet
This amulet, showing the thrones of Upper and Lower Egypt, is the symbol for the jubilee festival. This celebration renewed the pharaoh's power as well as their divine status.

1 Ropes

These ropes allow the boat to be towed along by officials when it is not being rowed.

2 Sun disc

This disc represents the Sun and shows the lotus flower from which it emerges each dawn.

3 Malqata

Next to the harbour is a grand festival palace complex, which we know as Malqata.

4 Celebrants

The king's female relatives celebrate by shaking sistrum rattles, filling the air with noise.

5 Rowers

Four rowers power the boat. They will move it out into the harbour and then around it.

6 Golden boat

The boat is richly decorated, covered in gold and intricately carved decorations.

7 Holy scent

A priest burns incense. This is part of the religious ceremony in which the king becomes a god.

8 Pharaoh

Amenhotep III is bedecked in golden jewellery and wears a patterned jubilee robe.

9 Queen Tiye

Tiye is Amenhotep's chief wife. She stands proudly beside him on the gleaming barge.

10 Canopy

A canopy shades the royal couple, keeping them cool despite the heat of the Sun.

11 Helmsmen

Two helmsmen stand at the rear of the boat. Their job is to steer its course.

A JUBILEE CELEBRATION

Today is the beginning of Pharaoh Amenhotep III's first Heb Sed celebration. Courtiers and foreign officials have gathered to celebrate 30 years of the pharaoh's reign. The pharaoh and his queen will begin their journey on a sparkling golden barge, before being carried in chairs to his funerary temple.

A HUMAN GOD

The glittering grandeur of Amenhotep III's jubilee festival was not without purpose. It aimed to show the world how great and glorious the pharaoh was and show off his wealth and power. But it also went a step further, and marked the moment when Amenhotep became the early form of the Sun god Aten.

Voyage through the Underworld

The barge journey that Amenhotep III made around his harbour symbolized the journey the Sun god Ra made through the underworld each night.

Ra journeyed on a golden boat just like the barge of Amenhotep III.

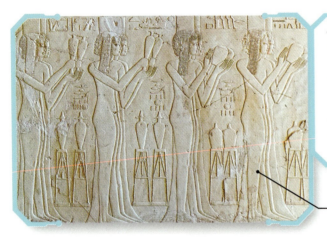

Storytelling walls

We know how Amenhotep III celebrated his jubilee because the event was recorded in carvings etched on the walls of a number of temples and tombs, including that of his wife's steward and scribe, Kheruef.

This scene shows Amenhotep's female relatives playing music at his jubilee festival.

The disc at the prow of the boat is made of pure gold.

The barge's bow is decorated with colourful patterns and symbols such as the Eye of Horus, which was believed to offer protection.

The priest is honoured by his role in the ritual. He must be careful to perform his duties well.

Workmen moved the equivalent of four Great Pyramids of sand in order to dig out the harbour.

The oarsmen must row in unison so the barge gildes smoothly through the harbour.

Engineering work

Amenhotep III built a colossal harbour to connect his palace to the Nile. Workmen dug out 11 million cubic metres (14 million cubic yards) of sand, earth, and gravel. The mounds they left behind are still visible.

Ceremonial wear

Particular items of clothing and jewellery were worn for ceremonial occasions in ancient Egypt. Menat necklaces were items of jewellery but could also be used like rattles, creating a sound intended to calm the gods.

The falcon is a symbol of Horus, the god of kinship and the sky.

This symbol is called an ankh. It represents life and was often used to suggest the pharaoh's power over life and death.

The helmsmen are barefoot, as is everyone on board besides the pharaoh and queen.

Amenhotep III holds a hooked crook and a flail. From ancient times, the Egyptians considered these farming tools to be symbols of justice and kingship.

Queen Tiye stands solemn and still. She plays a vital role in the complex ceremonies in which her husband will become a god.

THE PHARAOH'S TEMPLE

By the time of his first jubilee festival, Amenhotep III's grand funerary temple, Kom el-Hetan, was nearly complete. This temple was where his soul would be worshipped after death. He also used it to celebrate his three jubilee festivals. Some monuments, such as these colossal statues of Amenhotep III, still stand (or rather, sit) at the site today.

FACE OF A PHARAOH
Although there isn't much left to see of the palace at Malqata, there are many statues to show what Pharaoh Amenhotep III, who lived there, looked like. This enormous statue, now in the Egyptian Museum in Cairo, once stood in his funerary temple. It shows Amenhotep sitting together with his principal wife, Queen Tiye.

CARTHAGINIAN HARBOUR

In the 3rd century BCE, the city-state of Carthage was the great naval power of the Mediterranean. First founded by Phoenician, or "Punic", traders, it had a mighty harbour, home to hundreds of warships and merchant vessels. But between 264 and 146 BCE, Carthage fought and lost the Punic Wars with Rome. Its navy was destroyed and its generals, including the famous Hannibal, defeated. The Romans occupied Carthage, making it a new part of the Roman Empire.

Centre of the Mediterranean
The capital of the Carthaginian Empire, Carthage is not far from Tunis, the capital of modern Tunisia. It was founded in the 9th century BCE by Punic settlers from modern-day Lebanon.

Roman remains
After Carthage was finally defeated by Rome in 146 BCE, the city was virtually destroyed. Rome later colonized and rebuilt the city. Most ruins and mosaics remaining in Carthage today date from its Roman era, around the 4th or 5th century CE.

Deer are shown drinking from the Fountain of Life in this Roman mosaic found in Carthage.

Protective masks
Masks found at the site are believed to be the death masks of wealthy Carthaginians. The faces were designed to be ugly, with scary grinning expressions, because their job was to frighten away evil spirits in the underworld.

The masks were also sometimes used for plays and theatre performances.

Mediterranean mix
As a seafaring civilization, the Carthaginians came across aspects of other cultures that they mixed with their own. For instance, Melqart, the Carthaginian god of agriculture, merged over time with Herakles, the mythical Greek hero, to become Herakles-Melqart.

Cave temple and tombs
Known as the Tophet, this burial site close to the harbour is the oldest known place of worship devoted to Carthage's chief god, Baal, and his wife, the chief goddess, Tanit. It is thought that human sacrifices were carried out here.

Statue of the god Herakles-Melqart

The peak of Djebel Bou Korbous rises up to just over 400 m (1,300 ft). It is located on the peninsula that juts out on the other side of the Gulf of Tunis, the large but protected bay where Carthage was founded.

Tunis's Oceanographic Museum is located on the old harbour site, charting the city's long naval history.

The old *cothon*, or circular dock building, is long gone. All that remains is a grassy island and an archaeological site.

Traces of a harbour
The old harbour outline and the island where the *cothon* stood can still be seen among Carthage's modern buildings. But since the original Punic city was destroyed by the Romans, and the Roman city was torn down by Arab invaders in the late 600s CE, few ancient remains are left today. Some crumbling foundations of a Carthaginian housing district still stand on Byrsa Hill, from which this photograph of the old harbour was taken.

Model port
This modern model shows the ancient port at around 200 BCE. The circular dock, called the *cothon*, was only for military ships; an ancient writer claimed it could hold 220 vessels. The harbour leading into it was used by the trading ships that added to the city's growing wealth.

The top of the *caduceus* is formed by a pair of writhing snakes.

Blending symbols
This Carthaginian *stela*, a kind of tombstone, combines local and Roman influences. The figure in the middle is the Carthaginian goddess Tanit, but either side of her is a *caduceus*, the rod carried by the Roman god Mercury.

SETTING SAIL

Ships known as quinqueremes emerge from Carthage's military harbour on their way to confront the Romans at the Battle of Ecnomus in 256 BCE. As the ships pass through the commercial harbour, fishermen unload their catch, traders sell their wares, and men, women, and children from all over North Africa and the Mediterranean go about their daily lives in one of the busiest ports in the world.

Beardy beads
Carthage was famous for its glass-making. Glass bead pendants like this, showing the face of a man with curly hair and beard, were popular, and traded both at home and abroad. They are often found inside Carthaginian graves, as the dead were often buried with some of their finest possessions.

Unlike Roman coins, this one from Carthage has no writing describing what it depicts.

Carthaginian cash
The traders would have seen coins such as this Carthaginian half-shekel. It shows the god Melqart (or possibly the great general Hannibal) on one side, and one of Carthage's much feared war elephants on the other.

Local pottery
The city's pottery workshops produced amphorae (storage jars), household items, and incense burners such as this one, dating from around 150 BCE. It would have been used in religious ceremonies, with the incense placed in the top.

The carving depicts Baal-Hammon ("fiery Baal"), Carthage's chief god.

Feeding time
Babies in Carthage might have had one of these feeders – the vessel's "nose" is where the child drank from. The hair and large eyes painted on it represent Baal's wife Tanit, the mother-goddess of Carthage.

1 Fresh fish
A fishmonger and a soldier haggle over a fish. Caught locally, it still smells fresh.

2 Swords for hire
These men from Gaul and Germania in the north are mercenaries in Carthage's army.

3 Harbour master
Men in the raised area above the *cothon* guide ships in and out, as the fleet admiral watches.

4 Parking space
The circular *cothon*, or military harbour, can hold as many as 220 warships in its bays.

5 Strong defence
The military harbour's high walls and narrow entrance make enemy attacks impossible.

6 Armour plating
Shields are fixed along the ship railings to protect the troops from Roman arrows.

7 Free spot!
The harbour quays are lined with sturdy bollards for commercial ships to moor at.

8 Lookout post
Soldiers look out over the water, scanning it for any foreign ships approaching.

The *corvus*, a hooked ladder used to "grab" enemy ships and board them, was a Roman invention.

The square sails were tied up when not in use.

No one knows for sure, but the rowers were probably arranged with two on the top bench, two in the middle, and one on the bottom.

Inside a quinquereme

The main Carthaginian – and Roman – warship was a quinquereme. This meant there were five (*quinque* in Latin) oarsmen for each set of three oars. These ships were a faster, heavier upgrade on the Greek trireme, which only used three (*tria* in Latin) rowers per three oars.

Seafaring peoples

This carving of a ship was found in Phoenicia (modern-day Lebanon), the land that the people who first founded Carthage came from. Both Phoenicians and, later, Carthaginians depended on ships to expand their trade and influence.

WAR GALLEY

In the ancient world, whoever had the best fleet controlled the Mediterranean. No navy was better than that of Carthage, the North African empire whose super weapon was the quinquereme. Powered by 300 oarsm these ships were virtually invincible. That is until they came up against the equally invincible quinqueremes of Rome's navy. These two mighty empires clashed in many fierce sea battles, until Carthage was defeated

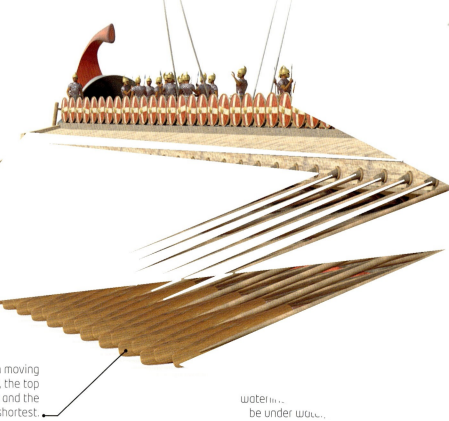

The oars were probably made of cedar wood.

To avoid clashing when moving in and out of the water, the top row of oars was longest and the bottom row shortest.

waterli
be under wat

The ship had masts, but its sails were only used if there was enough wind, and if the wind was blowing in the right direction. If not, the ship was propelled by rowing.

BATTLE OF DREPANA

The Battle of Drepana in 249 BCE, during the First Punic War (264–241 BCE), took place off Sicily. The Romans tried to trap the Carthaginian fleet in the harbour but they failed and the Carthaginians counterattacked. The Romans learned from the defeat, and, in the end, won the Punic Wars.

War helmet

Carthaginians wore different styles of helmet. This example, recovered off the coast of North Africa, was the simplest and most popular. It is called an Iberian helmet, as it originated in Iberia (in modern day Spain and Portugal) where Carthage had colonies.

This part of the ram attached to the front of the ship.

Ram to the slaughter

The front of each warship was fitted with a bronze battering ram. They weighed about 200 kg (440 lb) and sat just below the waterline. If they scored a direct hit, an enemy ship could sink in minutes.

Cheek guards could be attached here, but these have been lost or dissolved in the sea.

Most ships had eyes painted on the prow. Ancient people believed this meant the gods could see the way ahead and protect the vessel.

This is called a "fork" ram because it has three prongs, like a trident or a simple fork.

RAM RAIDERS

Marine archaeologists have recovered at least 25 Carthaginian and Roman battering rams, such as this one, from the seas off Sicily and other battle sites of the Punic Wars. In ancient times, the Romans kept the rams of captured ships as war trophies, displaying them in public in Rome.

A CITY IN THE ROCK

In the bleak, stony desert of southwestern Jordan lies a narrow canyon. Squeeze through it and you will arrive at Petra – a city partly carved out of the rock. Petra was built by the Nabateans, a nomadic people who organized a lucrative trading empire from this site, around two thousand years ago.

Desert city
The city of Petra was located in the desert, in an area that is now southern Jordan. It was the capital of the Nabatean Empire, positioned between Egypt, Arabia, and Syria-Phoenicia.

Caravan park
Groups of camels called caravans carried valuable trade goods across the desert to Petra. Camels are ideally suited to desert travel as they can carry large loads and go great distances without water.

This statue of a camel and its two riders is made of silver.

Masters of trade
Petra's strategic location allowed the Nabateans to control local trade. Traders could find shelter, food, and water in the city – for a price. These coins from 58 BCE show a camel and a king named Aretas.

Rocky capital
Petra was a large and thriving city. It contained shops, temples, tombs, a theatre, administrative buildings, and gardens. Some of the buildings were carved into rock, others were freestanding.

This carving shows a goddess, possibly al-Uzza, known as "the Mighty One".

Gods of Petra
The Nabateans worshipped many gods, including a few Greco-Roman deities, too. Each god had different attributes, such as power over water or fertility. Images of gods and goddesses were carved into rocks.

The Treasury

The most famous of the buildings carved into the rock at Petra is a royal tomb known as al-Khasneh, "the Treasury". The name comes from a tale told by the local Bedouin people that the Pharaoh of Egypt hid his gold in Petra. It is the most elaborately decorated building in the city, carved in Greco-Roman style. It was originally painted white, with colourful details.

1 Carved deities

Statues of goddesses such as Isis and Nike look out from the upper section of the 39-m (128-ft) tall façade.

2 Burial chambers

There are four burial chambers within the building but no human remains have been found there.

Hidden in the rock

Petra was a secret known only to the Bedouin people until the city was visited by Europeans in 1812. Interest spread rapidly, and foreign artists came here to capture the fascinating site.

TRADE CAPITAL

It has been a long, hard day of travelling, and the merchants of this caravan are weary. As they ride their camels through the canyon on the approach to Petra, buildings rise up dramatically in front of them, carved into the red sandstone of the canyon walls. The travel-worn traders pause to marvel at them, before continuing into the city for water, food, and rest.

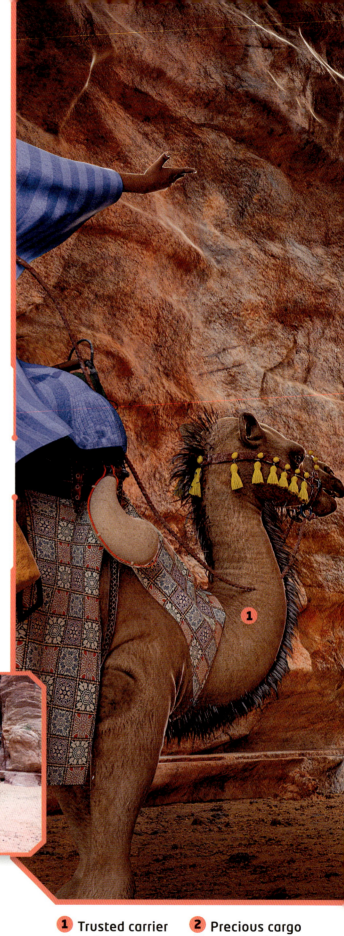

1

Fusion of cultures
The Nabataeans who built Petra took ideas from the many foreign merchants who passed through here. Some buildings have Eastern features, such as these Asian elephants on the Great Temple.

Sought-after sap
Frankincense is dried sap from a particular tree, which makes a sweet smell when it is burned. It only grows in a few places, including southern Arabia. The main route between those lands and the cities of the Mediterranean ran through Petra.

Ancient altar for burning incense

Important incense
The frankincense traded in Petra was used to make incense that was burned on altars across the ancient world. Its rarity and importance in religious ritual meant the Nabataeans were able to charge high tolls on its trade.

Desert plumbing
To transport water around their desert city, the Nabataeans built a sophisticated water storage and distribution system. It featured channels, underground cisterns, reservoirs, and pipes.

1 Trusted carrier
After a long journey through the desert, this camel will enjoy a drink of Petra's fresh water.

2 Precious cargo
The merchant's bags are full of expensive frankincense and myrrh used for incense.

3 First riders
This is just the head of the caravan, another 60 camels are following on close behind.

4 Impressive sight
Al-Khasneh towers over the riders as they wend their way past it towards the city.

5 Splash of colour
Brightly painted friezes and statues make the façade stand out against the rock.

6 Smaller inside
The chambers carved into the rock behind the grand façade do not match it at all in size.

7 Wrapped up
It is blisteringly hot, but the traders' robes and head wraps protect them from the Sun.

8 Money minded
This merchant is glad to be here but thinks about the tolls he has to pay before he can rest.

WINDING WAY

The main route into Petra goes through a narrow canyon, only 3 m (10 ft) wide in places. The 80-m (260-ft) tall sandstone rocks, formed millions of years ago, loom over the path, at some points almost touching overhead. The passageway is a natural formation, but the water channels along its base were carved by hand.

HOLY HILL

High above the Greek city of Athens, on a fortified hill known as the Acropolis, stands a collection of imposing temples and sanctuaries built over 2,000 years ago. At the centre of the Acropolis lies the Parthenon, a magnificent temple to Athena, the Greek goddess of war and wisdom who was Athens' favourite deity.

Heart of Greece
Many Greek cities had an acropolis, but the largest is in the centre of Athens, the country's modern capital. Athens is in a region of Greece known as Attica.

Nike co... Athens' military vic...

The series of fortified gates guarding the Acropolis is called the Propylaea.

Athenian leader
Most of the temples on the Acropolis were built during the time of Pericles, one of Athens' leading citizens in the period from 461–429 BCE. Pericles wanted his city's buildings to symbolize the power and influence of Athens. When it was finished in 432 BCE, the Parthenon was the grandest temple in the Greek world.

"Pericles" spelt in Greek letters.

Victory vase
This vase shows Athena armed with a shield. Winners at Athens' athletic games in the Panathenaia were given up to 40 of these vases filled with expensive olive oil. They could sell the oil and keep the earnings as prize money.

Under fire
By the 1400s, Athens was part of the Ottoman Empire (see page 157). In 1687, a cannonball fired at the Parthenon, which was being used as a mosque, hit a gunpowder store and severely damaged the ancient temple.

This marble seat was probably used by a priest.

Fallen columns
The Parthenon explosion of 1687 left columns lying where they fell. Fires and earthquakes have also caused parts of the Parthenon and the Acropolis's other buildings to collapse.

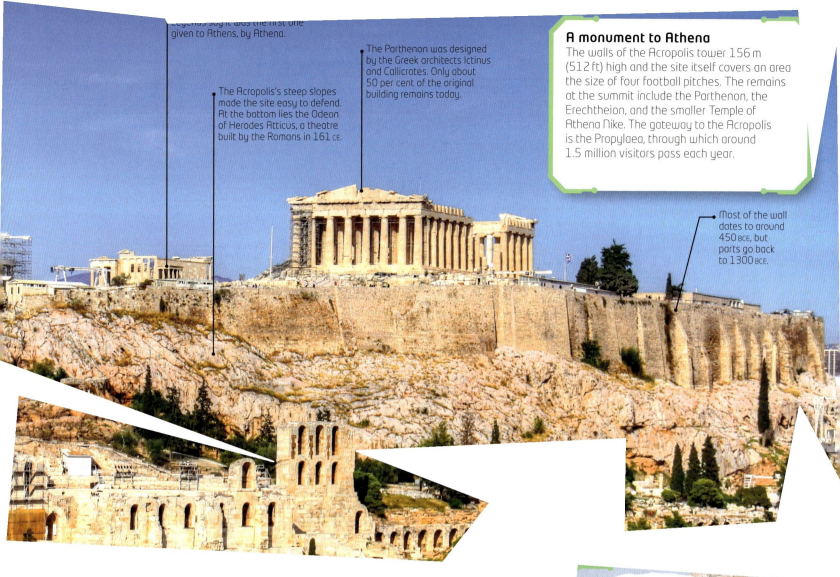

...legends say it was the first one given to Athens, by Athena.

The Parthenon was designed by the Greek architects Ictinus and Callicrates. Only about 50 per cent of the original building remains today.

The Acropolis's steep slopes made the site easy to defend. At the bottom lies the Odeon of Herodes Atticus, a theatre built by the Romans in 161 CE.

A monument to Athena

The walls of the Acropolis tower 156 m (512 ft) high and the site itself covers an area the size of four football pitches. The remains at the summit include the Parthenon, the Erechtheion, and the smaller Temple of Athena Nike. The gateway to the Acropolis is the Propylaea, through which around 1.5 million visitors pass each year.

Most of the wall dates to around 450 BCE, but parts go back to 1300 BCE.

Controversial sculptures

In 1801, Lord Elgin, Britain's ambassador to the Ottoman Empire in Constantinople, was granted permission to remove many of the Parthenon's sculptures. He said this was to save them from destruction. The sculptures are now in the British Museum, but there is a campaign to return them to Greece.

Hole allowed for a metal bridle to be fixed to the sculpture.

Conservation work

An umbrella protects this craftsperson from the hot sun while they work on restoring the porch of the Erechtheion temple on the Acropolis. The columns of the porch are designed to look like sculptures of young women.

FESTIVAL OF ATHENA

On a warm summer's day, the highlight of Athens' quadrennial festival of sports and music honouring its patron goddess Athena takes place: the Great Panathenaia Procession. Athenians march through the main square, the Agora, to the Acropolis to offer gifts and sacrifices to Athena.

1 Holy hill
The Acropolis, with its temples including the Parthenon, towers over the Greek city of Athens.

2 Ceremonial ship
A replica *trireme* ship on wheels is dragged through the city towards the Acropolis's slopes.

3 Titanic battle
The sail depicts the *gigantomachia*, a battle between the Greek gods and the *gigantes* race of giants.

4 From sail to shawl
The sail converts to a *peplos*, or shawl, which will be dedicated to Athena on the Acropolis.

5 Trays of treats
Metics, non-Greeks living in Athens, carry trays of cakes and honeycomb to honour Athena.

6 Military escort
Hoplites (Athenian soldiers) in full battledress escort the procession across the city.

7 In the lead
Girls called *kanephoroi* ("basket carriers") from rich Athenian families lead the procession.

8 Festival competitor
A Panathenaic Games athlete rides bareback – without saddle or stirrups – in the procession.

9 Holy water
Hydraiphoroi ("water carriers") transport the water used in the procession's animal sacrifices.

10 Marching to the beat
The music of the *aulos* (flute), *kithara* (lyre), and hand drums fills the air.

11 Keeping cool
Skiaphoroi ("umbrella carriers") hold parasols to protect the *kanephoroi* from the hot sun.

THE PARTHENON

The people of Athens arrive at the top of the Acropolis hill as the Panathenaia Procession reaches its end. Soon, the ceremonies celebrating the city's patron deity Athena will begin. Cattle are sacrificed in her honour and offerings to her are made.

The triangular top of the Parthenon is called the pediment. Most Greek and Roman temples have them.

The sculptures on the front, or east, pediment show how Athena was born, fully grown, dressed, and armed, from the forehead of her father, Zeus.

Anthemion
The decoration in the middle of the Parthenon's roof was called the anthemion. It was sculpted in the shape of a palm leaf and it stood 4 m (13 ft) tall.

The Parthenon's sculptures are brighly painted, with figures wearing colourful clothes.

All 46 outside columns are "fluted", or ridged, and decorated at the top in the simple Doric design.

Cheating the eye
When a structure is very long and wide it can appear to bow inwards. The Parthenon's builders knew this, so they made its columns and floor bulge outwards slightly to compensate for this optical illusion. So, despite looking straight, the Parthenon is curvy.

"Earth proudly wears **the Parthenon** as the best gem upon her zone."

- Ralph Waldo Emerson, 19th-century American writer and thinker -

Athens' greatest sculptor

Phidias (c. 490–430 BCE) designed the Parthenon's sculptures and friezes. He worked with the Parthenon's architects, Ictinus and Callicrates, to make one of the most perfectly proportioned and symmetrical buildings ever constructed.

These carvings, called a frieze, show processions honouring the gods.

The sculptures, or *metopes*, around the outside show stories from Greek legend, such as the fall of Troy.

Building the Parthenon

Workmen hauled marble and stone blocks 16 km (10 miles) from quarries outside Athens and then up the steep Acropolis hill. Wooden cranes lifted the stones, while craftsmen on wooden scaffolding fixed the blocks in place.

Athena holds a statue of Nike, the Greek goddess of victory.

This replica statue is based on a description of the original. The helmet is decorated with a sphinx with winged horses on either side.

The shield is carved with scenes from Greek mythology on both sides.

Sacred money

The goddess Athena was the symbol of Athens. Her face appeared on one side of the city's coins, and her symbol, the owl of wisdom, on the other.

Athena Parthenos

A statue known as Athena Parthenos dominated the interior of the Parthenon. It stood 11.5 m (38 ft) high and was made of gold and ivory panels around a wooden frame. It was created by the sculptor Phidias.

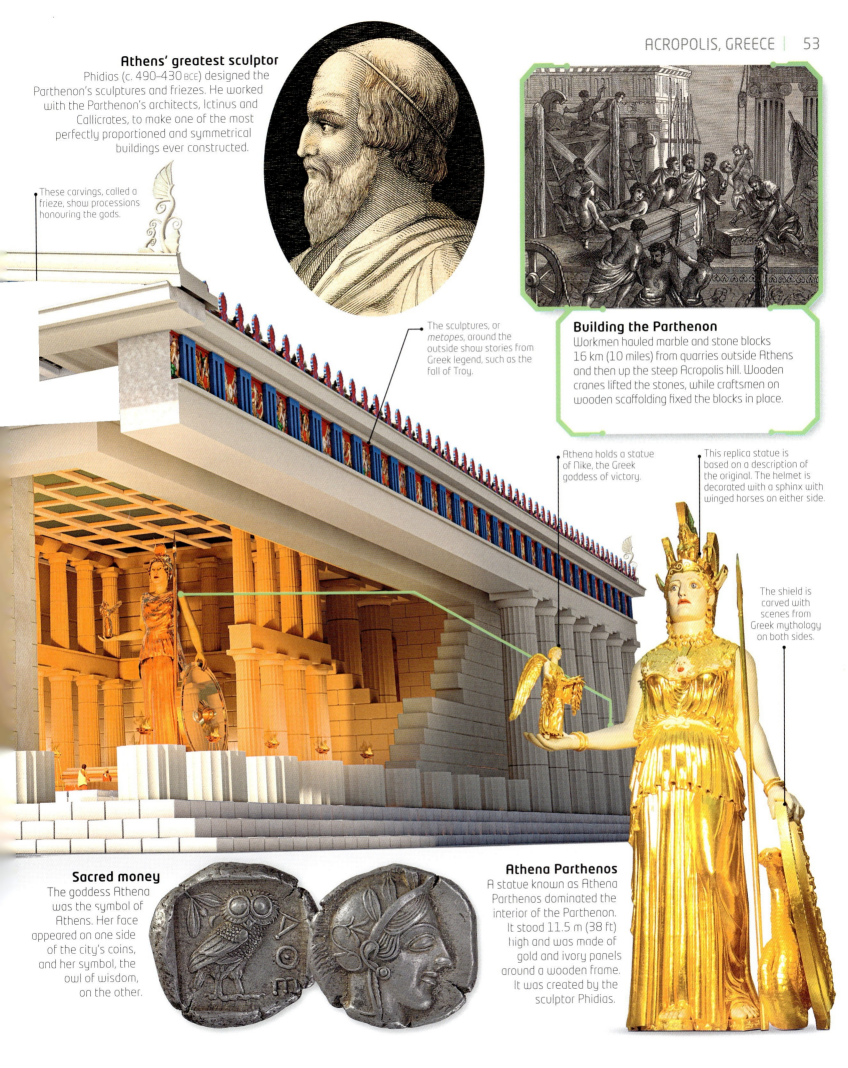

A TRIP TO THE THEATRE

The audience is sitting comfortably in the great open-air auditorium below the Acropolis. A god "flies" through the air as the action begins in one of Athens' favourite pastimes in the 4th century BCE: a day out at the theatre.

Birthplace of drama

The world's first-ever theatre was built on the slopes of the Acropolis and parts of it are still visible. The theatre was enlarged many times over its 800 years of use. It could fit 19,000 people.

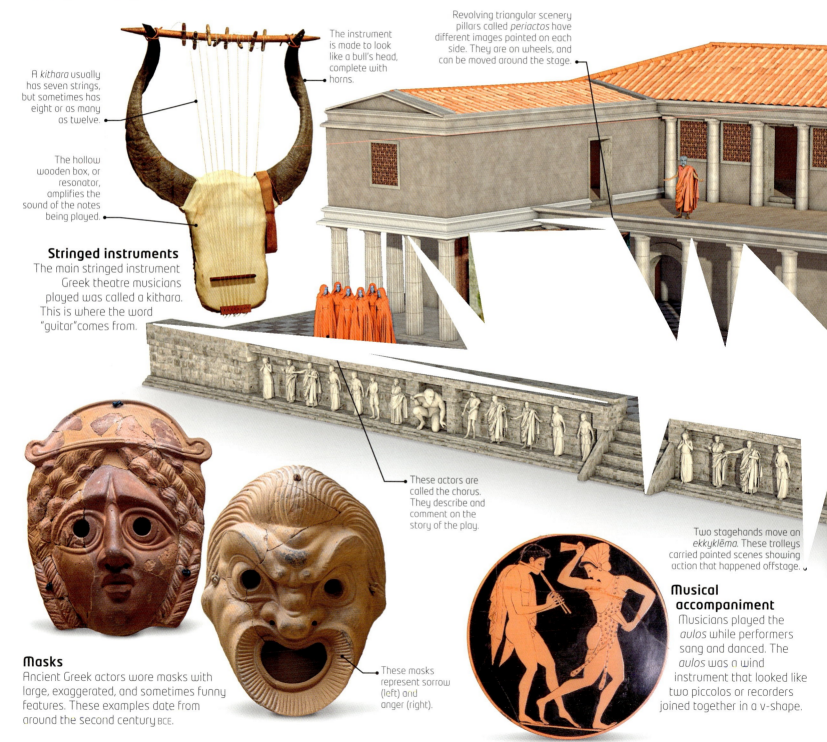

A *kithara* usually has seven strings, but sometimes has eight or as many as twelve.

The hollow wooden box, or resonator, amplifies the sound of the notes being played.

The instrument is made to look like a bull's head, complete with horns.

Revolving triangular scenery pillars called *periactos* have different images painted on each side. They are on wheels, and can be moved around the stage.

Stringed instruments

The main stringed instrument Greek theatre musicians played was called a kithara. This is where the word "guitar" comes from.

These actors are called the chorus. They describe and comment on the story of the play.

Two stagehands move an *ekkyklēma*. These trolleys carried painted scenes showing action that happened offstage.

Masks

Ancient Greek actors wore masks with large, exaggerated, and sometimes funny features. These examples date from around the second century BCE.

These masks represent sorrow (left) and anger (right).

Musical accompaniment

Musicians played the *aulos* while performers sang and danced. The *aulos* was a wind instrument that looked like two piccolos or recorders joined together in a v-shape.

The god Dionysus

Dionysus was the god of wine and transformation. In Athens he was also the god of drama, and at the Theatre of Dionysus plays and dances were performed in his honour, with the subject matter often drawn from mythology.

The inside of this *kylix* (drinking cup) shows Dionysus with grapevines growing from the mast of his ship.

A crane is used to lower an actor playing a god onto the stage. It is called a *deus ex machina*, meaning "god from the machine"

Seat of honour

While most of the theatre-goers sat on flat seats, the high priest of Dionysus had a special marble chair in front of the stage. There were 66 other *proedria* (seats of honour) reserved for special guests.

Stagehands make sure that the props are ready and in the right place, and help the performers get changed in between scenes.

Forming a backdrop, this part of the stage is called the *skene*. It also functions as an offstage area where actors get ready and where scenery, machinery, and musical instruments are stored.

The stage, or *proskenion*, is raised above the ground so that the audience can see the leading actors. The performers also wear high-heeled platform shoes, to make sure they are always visible.

The front of the stage

The stage front, or *hyposcenium*, at the Theatre of Dionysus included a sculpture of a character playing the god Atlas holding up the sky.

WEIGHT ON THEIR HEAD

Like its neighbour the Parthenon, the temple known as the Erechtheion was sacred to Athena. Its best-known feature is the porch supported by six carved female figures known as caryatids. The sculptures in place today are replicas; the originals are held in museums for safe-keeping.

ROMAN COLOSSEUM

A symbol of the glory of the Roman Empire, the Colosseum has stood in Rome for almost 2,000 years. In the centuries between its first opening in 80 CE and the last recorded events there in the early 500s CE, it was an arena of violent entertainment, including gladiatorial combat and beast hunts. Today, the Colosseum, despite being a ruin, is one of the world's most recognizable buildings.

Imperial centre

The Colosseum lies in the centre of modern-day Rome. Today, Rome is the capital city of Italy but at the time when the Colosseum was built, Rome was the centre of the Roman Empire.

This gladiator has been caught in a net by his opponent.

All fights were overseen by a referee, called a *summa rudis*. He made sure the gladiators stuck to the rules.

Sporting superstars

Gladiator fights in the Colosseum did not often end in death. Gladiators were like today's tennis stars or footballers. It cost a lot of money to train, feed, and arm them, and they were valuable to their owners (many, but not all, gladiators were enslaved).

The Colosseum uncovered

As the outer wall and arena floor have been lost, it is possible to look "inside" the Colosseum's structure and see the two-storey network of corridors and rooms that run underneath the arena.

Emperor Vespasian

Building work on the Colosseum began under Emperor Vespasian around 70 CE. It was paid for by some of the estimated 50,000 kg (110,214 lb) of gold and silver his armies took from Jerusalem and the province of Judaea after they put down a rebellion there.

The Colosseum's ground floor features simple columns. The column designs become more and more complicated and decorative on each of the next two floors.

The Colosseum is the largest amphitheatre from the Roman world. When fully intact, it was 189 m (620 ft) long, 156 m (511.8 ft) wide, and 50 m (164 ft) high.

A wonder in ruins
Only one third of the original Colosseum structure remains. This makes it easier to see how it was constructed, especially the three main "rings" of walls surrounding the arena. Over the centuries, the Colosseum has suffered through earthquakes, wars and battles, and the looting of the marble and metal used in its construction to build houses and churches after the end of the Roman Empire.

The outside of the Colosseum was clad in travertine. Inside it was made of brick, limestone, concrete, and a light volcanic stone called tufa, or tuff.

Naval battle?
It is said the Colosseum was once flooded to host a sea battle called a *naumachia*. Some experts disagree, pointing out the difficulty of making the arena watertight.

"They stage **gladiatorial games**, and at the mob's **thumb's down** will **butcher a loser** for popularity's sake."

- Juvenal, Roman poet, *The Sixteen Satires* -

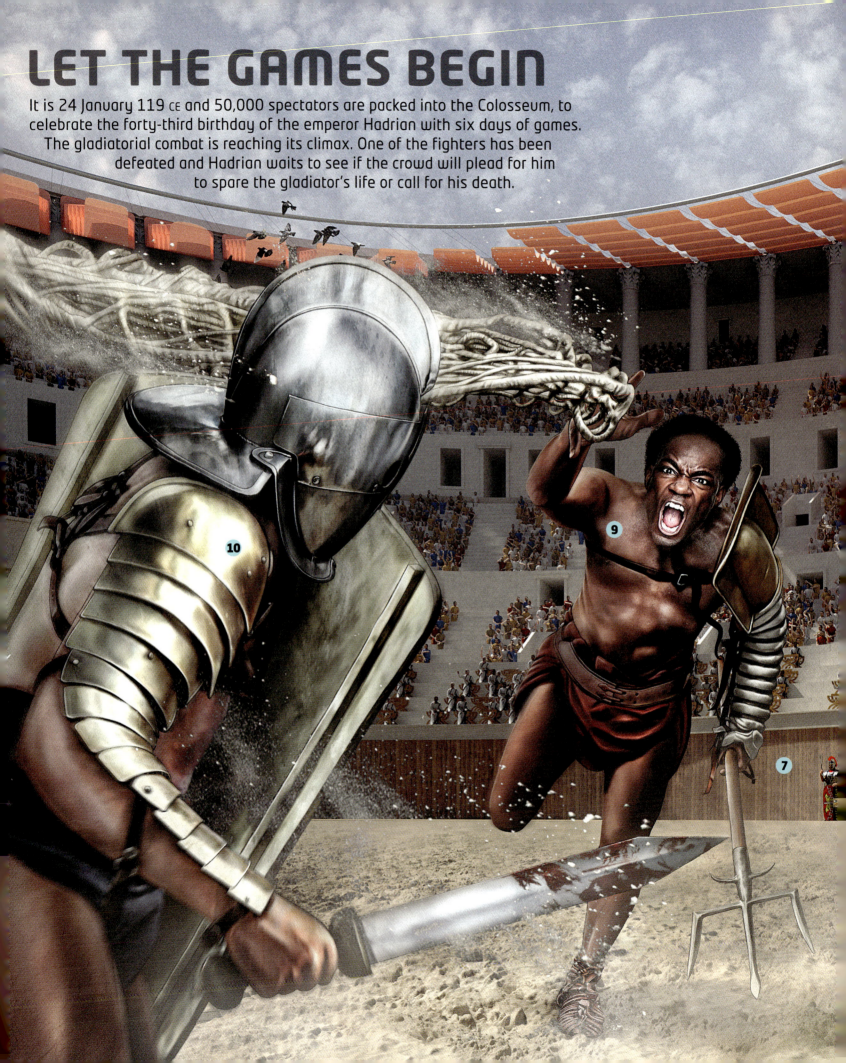

LET THE GAMES BEGIN

It is 24 January 119 CE and 50,000 spectators are packed into the Colosseum, to celebrate the forty-third birthday of the emperor Hadrian with six days of games. The gladiatorial combat is reaching its climax. One of the fighters has been defeated and Hadrian waits to see if the crowd will plead for him to spare the gladiator's life or call for his death.

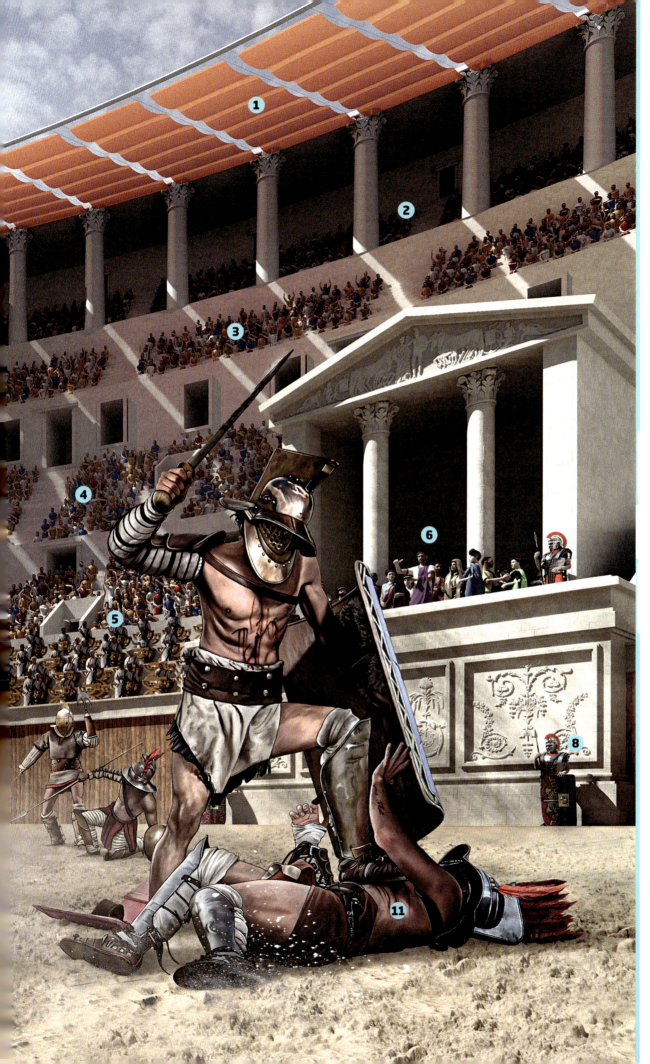

1 Velarium
This canvas shade can be rolled in or out to protect the crowd from the heat of the sun.

2 The top rows
These six rows at the top, with the worst view, are for women, and poor and enslaved people.

3 Seats for the plebs
Plebeians ("normal" citizens such as butchers and bakers) sit high up on wooden benches.

4 Middle tier
Middle-ranking men, known as equestrians, or knights, enjoy the action from halfway up.

5 Special seats
Senators and important guests from other cities or overseas sit closest to the action.

6 Royal box
Emperor Hadrian prepares to give judgement by raising a finger if the gladiator is to be spared.

7 Tall walls
3.7 m-high (12 ft) walls stop wild animals from escaping and savaging the spectators.

8 Armed guards
Legionaries guard the arena, in case any gladiators try to flee, or attack the emperor.

9 Retiarius
This gladiator's plan is to throw a heavy net over his opponent then spear him with his trident.

10 Secutor
Deflecting the net with his shield and then stabbing up is this gladiator's only hope.

11 To the death?
Gladiator matches rarely end in death. But this bout is special, and the emperor may call for it.

GLADIATOR COMBAT

The *Murmillo* gladiator has the upper hand as he stands over his rival, the *Thraex*, or "Thracian", named because their armour looked similar to that worn by people from Thrace in modern-day Bulgaria and Greece. Now the *Murmillo* waits to see if the emperor will allow him to spare his opponent's life.

The *gladius* is mainly used as a thrusting, stabbing weapon, but its sides are razor sharp, too.

The bronze helmet has a wide brim to protect the front and back of the head.

Fighters wear a roll of cloth covered with an iron or bronze arm guard, called a *manica*, fastened by leather straps to protect their sword or spear arm.

Gladiator training school
Just behind the Colosseum was the *Ludus Magnus*, a training arena and rooms where gladiators lived. It was connected to the Colosseum by an underground tunnel. This protected famous gladiators from being mobbed by fans if they were seen in public.

Belts can be 12–16 cm (4.7–6.3 in) wide and are made of thick folds of leather reinforced with bronze strips and studs.

Action figures
Gladiator-themed lamps, figurines, toys, statuettes, plates, cups, and even incense holders were very popular among ordinary Romans, who looked up to the highly-skilled fighters as their sporting heroes.

The Romans call leg guards *ocreae*. They are either leather or metal.

Gladiator Helmet
Known as a *cassis crista*, the *Murmillo* gladiator's helmet covered his whole face. This gave him lots of protection, but it was also hard to see out of, heavy, and slowed him down against more agile, lightly-armed fighters.

A horse-hair "tail" or a plume of feathers could be slotted into the helmet's crest.

The breastplate was fastened in place by thick leather straps at the shoulder.

Breastplate
Only one type of gladiator, the *Provocator*, wore a protective breastplate, or *cardiophylax*. He was supposed to look like a Roman legionary. All other gladiators fought bare-chested.

Sharp and deadly
Gladiators like the *Murmillo* carried a short sword called a *gladius*. It was the same type of weapon used by Roman legionaries. If a gladiator won his freedom he was awarded a wooden *gladius*-style sword known as a *rudis*.

Battle in stone
Gladiator contests were popular all over the Roman Empire. The inscription on this carving, for example, is Greek, indicating it is from a Greek-speaking part of the empire.

Scutum shields were 1.2 m (4 ft) long and made from three wooden boards stuck together and then covered in cloth and leather.

Leg defence
Most gladiators wore shin and knee guards, today known as greaves, to protect them from blows to their legs. Often, they would only wear them on their lead fighting leg – usually the right.

These ceremonial greaves are engraved. Gladiators usually wore plain leg guards..

The *Thraex*'s helmet is decorated with feathers. Some other gladiators fix horsehair "tails" to their helmets.

Sandals were known as *caligae*. They were thick-soled and very hard-wearing.

Roman sandals
Fighting in sandals could be a tricky business, as the gladiators' toes were exposed and unprotected. Some lucky fighters wore boots.

Strong shield
The *Murmillo*'s large, rectangular shield, called a *scutum*, weighed 10 kg (22 lb), making it hard to carry as fights wore on. It was the same type of shield that Roman legionaries used when they went into battle.

A DAY AT THE GAMES

Senators and enslaved people, police and thieves, shopkeepers, soldiers, noblewomen, and some very excited children: everybody's at the Colosseum today to see the gladiators in action. The fights are about to begin, but there is just enough time to buy some tasty snacks, chat with friends, and soak up the atmosphere before going in.

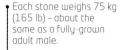

Each stone weighs 75 kg (165 lb) – about the same as a fully-grown adult male.

Every ground floor arch is numbered, so that spectators can find the entrance stamped on their "ticket".

Up to the terraces

Like a modern stadium, the Colosseum was designed with staircases and arched passages that meant it could be emptied of its 50,000 spectators in just 15 minutes.

Entrances to the stands are called *vomitoria*, because they are like large throats that "vomit" spectators in and out of the arena.

Wide, brightly-painted corridors provided plenty of space for crowds to move freely.

Staircases led up from the ground floor entrances to the higher seating levels.

A man scrawls graffiti inside the archway, possibly a message supporting his favourite gladiator.

Drinking water

There were up to 100 water fountains in and around the Colosseum. Water was supplied by Rome's aqueducts, and flowed off into the city's main sewer, the *Cloaca Maxima*.

As most Roman houses do not have running water, public fountains are many people's only water source.

Policemen of the *Cohortes Urbanae* escort an unruly citizen out of the arena. It's going to be a busy day for them.

Two senators parade in public, keen to show themselves as simple men of the people – despite their expensive togas!

Public toilets

This Roman toilet from Ostia near Rome is similar to the two large toilets at the Colosseum. There was no toilet paper, just a sponge on a stick in a bucket of water for everyone to share.

Tesserae tickets

Entry to the Colosseum was free and was awarded by lottery. "Tickets" were clay tokens called *tesserae*, and each one was marked with an archway entrance number and seat number.

These markings were probably scratched into the wall by a fan of the gladiatorial games.

Graffiti everywhere

The Colosseum, like many of Rome's buildings, had graffiti on its walls. This drawing of gladiators in combat comes from the city of Pompeii, to the south of Rome.

Praetorian guard

When VIPs such as the emperor and his family came to the Colosseum, his personal military troops, the Praetorian Guard, were there to protect them. They patrolled the stadium alongside the *Cohortes Urbanae*, Rome's police force.

The Colosseum is Rome's best begging spot. On a games day, people are happy and excited, and more likely to be generous.

A young pickpocket helps himself to a spectator's valuables. If he gets caught, he can expect to be beaten or flogged.

It is not known for sure, but girls were probably not allowed into the Colosseum. Boys could only sit in a special area with an adult.

Looking after the animals

One of the most dangerous jobs in the Colosseum was being one of the *bestiari*, the men controlling the wild animals. They had to make sure that the beasts could not escape and run loose in the *hypogeum*, and that they made it safely onto the arena floor.

BEHIND THE SCENES

As gladiators do battle and crowds enjoy the show, below the Colosseum floor, in the *hypogeum*, it's hot, noisy, and smelly. Fighters prepare for combat or tend to their wounds afterwards, while skilled animal handlers prepare the wild beasts for their entrance into the arena.

Exotic beasts

The Colosseum's tigers were imported from India, 6,500 km (4,039 miles) away. The journey by land and sea would have taken between two to three months. Some tigers were also taken from Turkey.

Tigers were usually brought to Rome as cubs. This made it easier and safer for traders to transport the most feared and vicious of all the Colosseum's wild animals.

The bear's eye socket may have been damaged in an arena fight or at some point after the animal's death.

Remains of a bear

This bear skull, from the 4th or 5th century CE, was found near the Colosseum. It is unusual, as most dead animals from the arena were buried in large graves outside Rome. Some were thrown into the River Tiber, or even eaten.

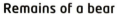

Two gladiators engage in combat. They prepared for the fight below the arena, in the dressing rooms of the *hypogeum*.

The arena floor is made of wooden boards. It is covered in sand to soak up the blood and gore.

Wild animals, such as lions, are kept in 32 iron cages. The cramped space makes them bored and angry – and ready to fight when the time comes.

Winches lift the cages up to ramps leading to the 36 trapdoors cut into the arena floor. The trapdoors spring open, allowing the beasts to rush out on the stage.

Bags of sand, animal feed, and other items are stored in the long, dark, winding corridors below the Colosseum.

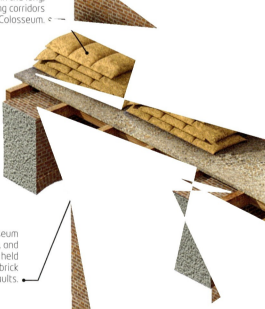

The whole Colosseum – inside, outside, and even underneath – is held up by hundreds of brick arches and vaults.

The lower of the *hypogeum*'s two levels has service corridors as well as drains which empty into Rome's sewers.

For special shows, such as re-enacting a scene from mythology, painted props help to create a sense of drama.

Venatores are gladiators specially trained to fight against wild animals.

A tiger leaps out through the trapdoor.

Reconstructed lift

In 2015, archaeologists and engineers rebuilt one of the Colosseum's wooden lifts. They tested it by lifting a wolf. It worked perfectly, rising 7.3 m (24 ft) to the arena floor. The lift uses the same materials and tools the Romans used. It took 18 months (and €20 million) to build.

HONEYCOMB STRUCTURE

The structure of the Colosseum is massive but not solid – this photograph of its interior reveals the many service rooms and passages under its long-gone stage floor. The arched entrances at each end lead into the arena. Encircling the arena are the vaulted passageways used by spectators to get to and from their seats.

ROCK PALACE

Sri Lanka's Sigiriya palace sits on the top of a pillar of rock, which looms over lush green forest – the rock towers 200 m (650 ft) taller above the landscape around it. The palace was built in the 5th century, by King Kashyapa. Caught up in a struggle for power, Kashyapa first killed his father and then fought his brother. He built Sigiriya as his new palace-capital, making sure it would be easy to defend in a battle.

Rock in the forest
Sigiriya sits at the northern edge of Sri Lanka's central highlands. The rock rises up from a forested area bordering several national parks.

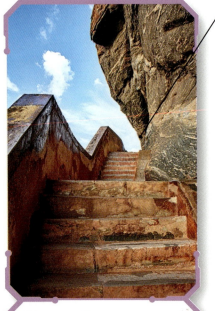

This section of the rock wall is covered in paintings of beautiful ladies (see page 73).

1 This large, rock-cut pool was used to store rainwater as well as being a decorative feature. The water that collected here was used for drinking and for watering the palace gardens.

Mirror wall
A steep path winds around the rock. The side of the wall is shiny, and reflects the paintings on the rocks that face it. This mirror wall is covered in graffiti, written by ancient tourists.

Well guarded
Beneath Sigiriya rock were several wide, deep moats. They were filled with crocodiles, to frighten off potential invaders. Crocodiles still live in the moats today.

King Ravana is described as having ten heads and twenty arms.

This solid plug of rock was once magma. It forms the rock we see today.

The rock that formed the outer layers of the volcano has slowly eroded away.

Volcanic plug
The rock on which Sigiriya stands is the remains of an ancient volcano, which last erupted over two billion years ago. Over time, the outer layers of the volcano eroded away, leaving behind only the hardened inner core.

Current ground level

Core of magma

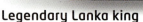

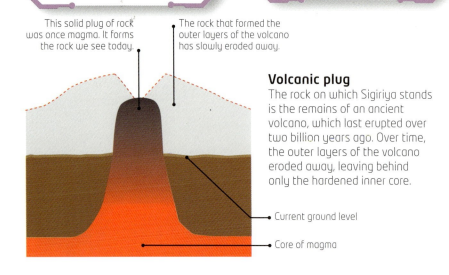

Legendary Lanka king
Ravana is one of the main characters in an ancient Hindu epic myth, the Ramayana. He was the king of Lanka, thought by many to be the island of Sri Lanka. Similarities between Sigiriya and descriptions of Ravana's legendary palace have led to some people linking the two.

High above it all

Evidence suggests that people have lived on Sigiriya rock since the 3rd century BCE. The palace was built in around 480 CE, but it was used as a palace for less than 15 years, ending with King Kashyapa's death in 495 CE. The buildings were then used as a Buddhist monastery, before being abandoned in the 14th century. Today, tourists scale the narrow steps up to the ruins at the top.

2 This throne was carved out of the rock around it. It faces east and was once shaded by a four-poster canopy.

3 The palace sits on the highest part of the rock. Built over several levels, it had a 360-degree view of the surrounding countryside.

4 The Lion Gate was the entrance to the fortress. It is thought to have been a sculpture of a whole lion, but today only two paws remain.

5 A series of gardens were built around the base of the rock, enclosed by moats. They featured many pools, streams, and water channels.

Lion gate

Halfway up the rock are two massive paws, known as the Lion Gate. The steps between the paws lead to the steep path that climbs up to the palace at the top of the rock.

1 Royal outing
King Kashyapa steps out beneath the lion's mouth, on his way to the gardens far below.

2 Good company
Some well liked and trusted members of the court accompany the king on his excursion.

3 Fresh fruit
Fruit and vegetables for the king's meals grow in the orchards planted on the rock's edge.

4 Pink petals
Lotus plants grow in the great pool. Their flowers are harvested and used in the palace.

5 Rehearsal
With the king out of earshot, musicians are practising for the evening's recital.

6 Stone throne
The king's stone seat has been polished and prepared for him to use tonight.

A ROYAL HIDEAWAY

Sri Lanka is in turmoil, and King Kashyapa has fled to Sigiriya after killing his own father. While in hiding, Kashyapa spends his days turning this monumental rock into paradise on Earth. This afternoon, he will take a stroll around the gardens, while the palace is being prepared for a music recital.

Buddhist beliefs

Buddhism has been the main religious belief in Sri Lanka for more than 2,000 years. Sri Lankan kings constructed stupas (shrines) and statues of the Buddha to show their religious devotion.

This giant Buddha, 14 m (46 ft) tall, was raised by Kashyapa's father, King Dhatusena. It stands in the village of Avukana, not very far from Sigiriya.

Premier seat

This seat was cut from the rock that surrounds it. It overlooks an open area, where recitals and plays took place. From here, the king would have had an excellent view.

The women wear valuable jewellery and elaborate hair decorations.

Tropical fruits

The women of Sigiriya

Paintings on the rock walls feature many women. They may have represented women of the court, or divine spirits, called apsaras.

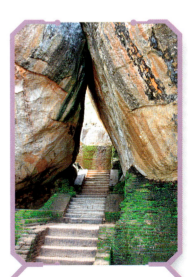

Boulder garden

There were several gardens at the foot of the rock, far beneath the palace. One of these gardens features huge boulders, with steps leading between them.

7 **Sneak peak**
Some members of the king's household have gathered to get a first look at the performers.

8 **Stupa**
A Buddhist structure called a stupa marks the highest point of the rock.

WATER GARDENS

The water features of the Sigiriya gardens are filled, and emptied, by an elaborate system of engineering. Water is collected in huge reservoirs, then gravity and pressure push it through underground pipes and into the pools and fountains. The system still works today, around 1,500 years after it was built.

MAYA CITY

The ancient city of Chichen Itza was built by the Maya people, in around the 6th century CE. The Maya have lived in this part of the Americas for thousands of years. Historically, the region was organized into city-states, each full of impressive buildings and controlled by its own all-powerful ruler. Astronomy, religion, and ballgames were key parts of Maya culture.

City-state ruins
Chichen Itza is in the modern-day Mexican state of Yucatán. The Maya region also included areas in Central America that today make up Guatemala, Belize, and parts of Honduras.

The top temple building contains two chambers.

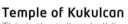

Temple of Kukulcan
This is the tallest building at Chichen Itza. The terraced platform – often called a pyramid – and the building at its top were built over an earlier structure. It is made from stone blocks, some of which have decorative carvings.

1 The Temple of Kukulcan is positioned towards the centre of the city. The 30-m (98-ft) tall structure has nine terraced platforms. Four staircases lead up to the top temple, one on each side.

2 The ballcourt was a sports arena, where the Maya competed in a ballgame. The ballgame was sacred – it was played to honour the gods.

Maya rulers
Each Maya city-state was headed by a single king or queen. These rulers were considered to have god-given powers, and to act as middlemen between their people and the gods. They controlled all the decisions in their city-state.

Snake heads
Carvings in the shape of snake heads can be seen in many Maya sites – they represent Kukulcan, a feathered snake god. The Maya worshipped Kukulcan as a creator god. They believed he controlled life and the weather.

This jade mask shows Pakal, ruler of the Palenque city-state.

Fierce snake heads are carved at the base of the stairs of the Temple of Kukulcan.

2

1

3

City in the jungle

The Maya seem to have abandoned Chichen Itza in around 1440 CE. The forest grew up around the unoccupied city, with plants hiding large parts of its buildings from view. In the 1880s, work was begun to uncover Chichen Itza. The vegetation was cleared back from some of the ruins, and the crumbling buildings were restored.

MAYA WOMEN

Fine jewellery shows that this is a wealthy woman.

Loom used for weaving fabrics

These columns would once have supported a roof.

3 The Temple of the Warriors has four square platforms, surrounded by hundreds of columns. Inside the temple is a carving that shows warriors, eagles, and jaguars.

Stone man

Sculptures of a man looking like he is resting, with a bowl on his stomach, appear throughout the Maya world. They may have been places where people could leave offerings for the gods.

In Maya society, women were able to become leaders and take part in government. They were also in charge of weaving fabrics used for clothes, an important activity often shown in art.

TEMPLE OF KUKULCAN

An eerie light falls over the city of Chichen Itza as the Moon passes between Earth and the Sun. This solar eclipse has long been predicted by the city's astronomers, and the people of the city-state have gathered at the Temple of Kukulcan to witness the spectacle. The king and his priests lead the excited crowd in prayer and religious rituals.

1 Solar eclipse
As the Sun disappears behind the Moon, it almost looks as if something is eating it.

2 Top temple
The holy temple is located right at the top of the pyramid. Only a few people are allowed up here.

3 Holy leaders
The king and priests have gathered at the entrance to the temple.

4 Sacred dress
The priests wear elaborate costumes garlanded with feathers for this occasion.

5 Holy smoke
Smoky copal incense is burned by the priests, as part of the ceremonial ritual.

6 Painted pyramid
The outside of the pyramid has been painted in bright, contrasting colours.

7 Nine layers
The layers of the pyramid stand for the nine different parts of the Maya underworld.

8 Many steps
Together, the four staircases have a total of 365 steps – one for each day of the year.

9 Here for the view
Elite fighters and other important people watch from the Temple of the Warriors.

10 Pilgrims
Hundreds of people have gathered to dance and worship at the foot of the pyramid.

11 Well dressed
People have dressed in their best, many wearing the finest turquoise jewellery.

The Great Ballcourt
Longer than a professional football (soccer) pitch, Chichen Itza's ballcourt is the largest one known in Mesoamerica. It is 168 m (551 ft) long, and 70 m (230 ft) wide.

Each side of the court has a stone ring embedded in it. The rings may have marked the centre of the court, as a net does in volleyball. Each team tries hard not to miss the volley.

The ball is a solid lump of rubber. It is heavy, with a slight bounce to it. Players are only allowed to strike the ball with their knees, elbows, and hips.

The players have made sure they look good for this important match. They wear padded belts and elaborate headdresses with plenty of feathers.

The court is rectangular. It has a flat floor, with steep walls along the two long sides. Each wall has a slope running along the bottom.

Popular all over

Versions of the ballgame were played across Mesoamerica. They all used a ball, hoops, and two teams. However, the shape, layout, and dimensions of the court changed from place to place, and probably the rules, too.

AT THE BALLGAME

The ballgame is underway, and players leap energetically across the court. The game is fast-paced and occasionally violent. Two teams compete, aiming to score points when the opposing side drops the ball. There's more at stake here than just winning or losing – the aim of the game is to honour the gods with impressive feats of athleticism.

This clay model shows a ballgame played by the Nayarit people, who lived in western Mexico.

At the northern end of the ballcourt is the Temple of the Bearded Man. People standing here have a clear view of what happens as the game unfolds.

The most important spectators watch the game from the temple. But the people jostling for space in the side stands, along the walls of the ballcourt, are often closer to the action.

Wrist protection

Knee pad

Layers of fabric would have lessened the hard rubber ball's impact on the body.

Player protection

The ballgame provided plenty of opportunities for players to get hurt. These ceramic figures are from Jaina Island in Mexico. They show players wearing thick protective clothing.

Knee pads help protect the players, allowing them to make risky moves they might not attempt otherwise.

The ballgame today

Versions of the ballgame are still played in Mexico and Central America today, with different rules in different areas. It is thought to be one of the oldest sports in the world, having been played continuously for around 3,500 years.

The tiny observation chamber is right at the top of the observatory.

Crumbling observatory

Today, the ruined round tower is clearly visible sitting on its square base, and the inner spiral staircase, leading to the observation chamber at the top. It is now known as "El Caracol" in Spanish, which means "The Snail", because it resembles a snail's shell.

The Sun is setting, turning the sky over Chichen Itza red and orange. Today is the spring equinox – the day and night will be exactly the same length.

This long shaft is used for viewing the planet Venus as it reaches its southernmost position.

WATCHING THE SKY

It is the spring equinox. As the Sun sets, light pours through a precisely-angled window of the observatory at Chichen Itza, brightening the room inside. An astronomer priest is here with his pupils to observe the phenomenon. The motion of the Sun, stars, and planets are of great significance to the Maya, whose calendars are based on astronomical movements.

The walls of the observation chamber are made of thick slabs of stone.

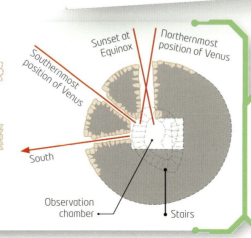

The observation chamber is reached by a spiral staircase that runs up the centre of the round tower.

A small group of selected students are listening to the priest.

Sunset at Equinox

Northernmost position of Venus

Southernmost position of Venus

South

Observation chamber

Stairs

Observation chamber

The chamber at the top of the observatory has a number of openings that are designed to align with certain astronomical events in the skies above. The openings give a person inside the observatory the perfect line of sight for watching each event.

The astronomer priest is about to explain how to use a forked staff to make observations.

Seeing Venus
The planet Venus was important in Maya astronomy. They recorded the planet's movements and seem to have associated it with war. The sign with four circles in the middle of this plate is the Maya sign for Venus.

Heavenly gods
Maya myths depict celestial bodies as deities with human-like features, with the Sun god the most significant. This ceramic jar shows the Maya Moon goddess, who is holding a rabbit.

MAYA SCRIPT

Maya writing used symbols called glyphs, seen here on a clay tablet. Some glyphs represented syllables and others whole words. They were laid out in blocks such as this one, which were read from left to right from top to bottom.

A key member in Maya society, this priest has a high status. He communicates with the gods, studies astronomy, and makes calendars.

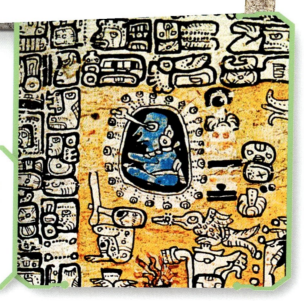

Astronomy book
The Maya wrote about astronomical observations and calendar events in documents now known as codices. Surrounded by Maya script, the blue figure on this codex page represents an astronomer looking at the sky.

TWO HUNDRED COLUMNS

Beside the Temple of the Warriors at Chichen Itza is a huge rectangular courtyard, dotted with two hundred columns. These would once have had a layer of plaster, painted in bright colours. Originally the columns supported a roof, but it is not known what this structure was used for.

BYZANTINE CHURCH

The huge dome of Hagia Sophia towers over the skyline of Istanbul. Once, Istanbul was called Constantinople, the capital of the Byzantine Empire – the part of the Roman Empire that survived after Rome fell to invaders in 476 CE. Hagia Sophia was originally built as a church, where the Byzantines worshipped the Christian god.

Name change
Constantinople became Istanbul in 1930. Home to Hagia Sophia, it is the largest city in Turkey. It straddles Europe and Asia, sprawling out on both sides of the Bosphorus Strait.

Justinian I built the current version of Hagia Sophia.

The Virgin Mary and Jesus receive gifts from the two emperors.

Constantine I was the founder of the city of Constantinople.

Divine emperors
The Byzantine empire was administered by Christian emperors, who were thought of as God's regents on Earth. This mosaic from Hagia Sophia depicts two of them next to the Virgin Mary and baby Jesus.

Roman races
Many Roman traditions took place in Constantinople. At the Hippodrome, charioteers raced horse-drawn chariots around the track, while the crowds shouted in support of their favourite teams.

This enamel cross shows the Virgin Mary, flanked by two saints.

Byzantine cross
The Byzantines were devout Christians. They created many forms of religious images, including icons. Featuring the Virgin Mary, Jesus, or the saints, these images were often very elaborate, like this pendant in the shape of a cross.

Constantinople
This illustration shows the prosperous port city in medieval times, protected by defensive walls. Constantinople was the capital of the Byzantine Empire until 1453, when it fell to the Ottoman Turks and became the capital of their empire.

From church to mosque

Hagia Sophia was built 1,500 years ago. When the Ottoman Empire overthrew the Byzantines, they changed the purpose of the building, turning it from a church into a grand mosque. In 1934, the Turkish Republic made the mosque into a museum. In 2020, Turkey's government decided to make Hagia Sophia into a mosque again.

The minarets were added by the Ottomans, after Hagia Sophia became a mosque in 1453.

The main dome is known as the cupola. The centre of the cupola is 56 m (184 ft) above the floor inside.

This building was once used to baptize people. It became the tomb of an Ottoman sultan in 1639.

Heavy stone buttresses support the building's weight.

A Mediterranean empire

The Byzantine Empire reached its greatest extent under Justinian I. He conquered a huge area of land around the Mediterranean Sea, much of which had once belonged to Rome. Over the centuries, its borders changed many times.

THE BYZANTINE EMPIRE

Constantinople

Mediterranean Sea

Extent of the Byzantine Empire at the death of Justinian I, in 565 CE

Grand interior

The inside of Hagia Sophia is centred around a vast, echoing space, crowned by a great dome. Byzantine Christian mosaics share the space with elements of Ottoman design, such as Islamic calligraphy.

1 Grand column
The steps of this towering column provide a great viewing platform.

2 Spectators
A noble couple watch the proceedings, happy to show off their fashionable clothing.

3 Flower petals
Handfuls of rose petals are thrown into the air, to celebrate the special occasion.

4 Shining building
The façade of the church is clad in white marble. It gleams brightly in the sunshine.

5 Stalls
Enterprising traders are on hand to sell food and souvenirs to the bustling crowd.

6 Clergyman
A priest leads the procession through the crowds and towards the church.

CORONATION DAY

It is 681 CE. Constantine IV has announced his 11-year-old son Justinian as co-emperor, to ensure that he will one day become emperor. Today the boy will be crowned. The father and son are on their way from the Great Palace to Hagia Sophia, where the ceremony will take place. There will be races at the Hippodrome, too!

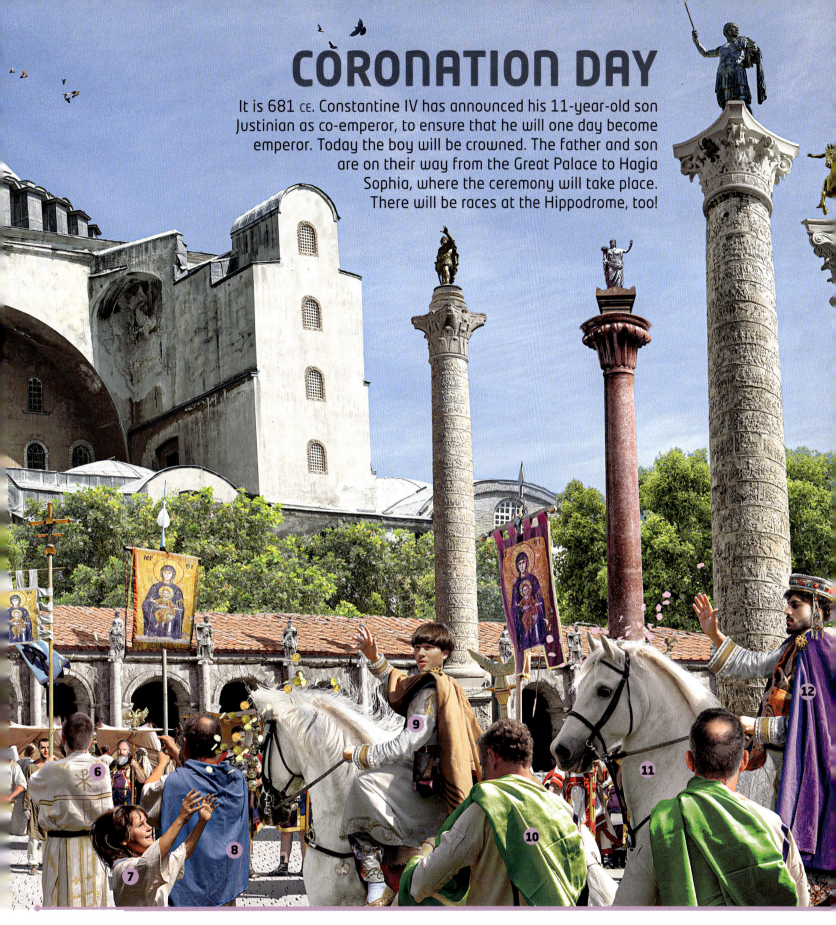

7 Lucky child
This child is very happy – she is about to catch a gold coin. Will she keep it or spend it?

8 Up the blues!
Wearing blue, this man supports the blue team of charioteers at the Hippodrome.

9 Justinian
Young Justinian throws coins into the crowd. He tries to act like an emperor-to-be.

10 Up the greens!
This man is a supporter of the green horse racing team, fierce rivals of the blue team.

11 Horses
The horses are the finest in the empire, but the noise is making them a bit nervous.

12 Constantine IV
The emperor rides beside his son. He is in full imperial costume, showing his authority.

CROWNED CO-EMPEROR

Emperor Constantine IV and his son have reached the hallowed interior of Hagia Sophia. The church is full of holy men, richly-dressed nobles, and the sweet scent of roses. Constantine has wrapped his son in a purple cloak to show his new status, and is about to place the crown itself on his head.

The cross and the top parts of this crown were added later on in medieval times.

Coronation crown
Byzantine imperial crowns were made of gold and covered in large gemstones. They also featured religious imagery, such as pictures of the Virgin Mary and various saints.

These dangling bejewelled chains are typical of Byzantine crowns.

1 The coronation takes place in a large raised pulpit, known as an *ambo*.

2 Musicians play to celebrate this holy historic moment.

3 The Patriarch, head of the Byzantine Church, is leading the coronation service.

4 Justinian is now dressed in the imperial purple cloak, called a *chlamys*.

5 Emperor Constantine IV places a crown on the head of his son, making him co-emperor.

The scent of roses
Roses were grown all over Constantinople, in the imperial gardens, and in grounds owned by Hagia Sophia. The flowers were used to make rose water, oil, perfume, and sweets, and to decorate the streets at coronations.

Looking good
Appearance was important to the Byzantines. Both men and women used hair dye, and lotions to soften their skin. Women also used makeup to draw around their eyes and lips, kept in jars like this one.

This cosmetics jar is made from gold, sapphire, and rock crystal.

6 The emperor's own guards are stationed at various spots to keep an eye on things.

Lighting up

Byzantine churches and homes were lit with oil lamps and hanging candelabras. Many of them were beautiful as well as functional, with elaborate decorations.

Chains were used to hang oil lamps from walls or ceilings.

Head of a griffin, a mythical beast

Empress Theodora

Fabulous finery

Wealthy Byzantines loved to wear fine jewellery and beautiful fabrics, especially at official occasions. This mosaic shows Empress Theodora (the wife of an earlier emperor, called Justinian I) and her ladies dressed in embroidered silks.

Coronation coins

All Byzantine rulers had their own coins made when they became emperor. This one was made when Justinian became sole emperor in 685, after his father died. He was only 16 years old when he became Justinian II.

7 The most important of Constantinople's holy men have gathered at Hagia Sophia today.

8 Some of the priests are kneeling on the cold, gleaming marble slabs that cover the church floor.

DIVINE DECORATION

Byzantine churches are richly decorated, with great expanses of marble, intricate mosaics, and golden religious icons. Here, workers are busy decorating the baptistery at Hagia Sophia. The baptistery is an important room in the church, as it is where people will come to be baptized. A large stone font has already been put in place in the middle of the room.

Baptistery font
This font is so large that people would have been able to walk into it, to be baptized with olive oil and water. It got moved from the baptistery into a courtyard when this room was turned into an Ottoman mausoleum (tomb).

This mason is carrying a load of building material on his shoulder.

Byzantine builders
The Byzantines built many churches and grand buildings all over their empire. These two builders are shown in a mosaic laid out in a church in 533, in what is now Jordan.

Many worked barefoot like this man, but the builder on the left is wearing boots.

Gold-leaf pieces were used as background and for crowns.

Shades of blue, turquoise, and green were the easiest to make.

Red glass was the hardest to produce.

Precious pieces
The tiny tiles used to make mosaics are called tesserae. The Romans had used mosaics to decorate their floors, using hard stones that people could walk on. Byzantine mosaics often decorated walls, so they could use more delicate materials, such as shiny gold-leaf and glittering glass in bright colours.

The large piece of marble in the middle is sliced from a column over 3 m (10 ft) in diameter.

Marvellous marble
Hagia Sophia is decorated with marble from all over the Byzantine Empire. In one part of its floor, the marble has been cut and laid to create patterns in a range of colours. It is also used for columns and wall panels.

ICONIC IMAGES

The Byzantine Church is known for its icons – images of the Virgin Mary, Jesus, and the saints. But in some periods, priests destroyed icons because they were worried that people would worship the icons rather than the holy people they depicted. This picture shows priests painting over an icon.

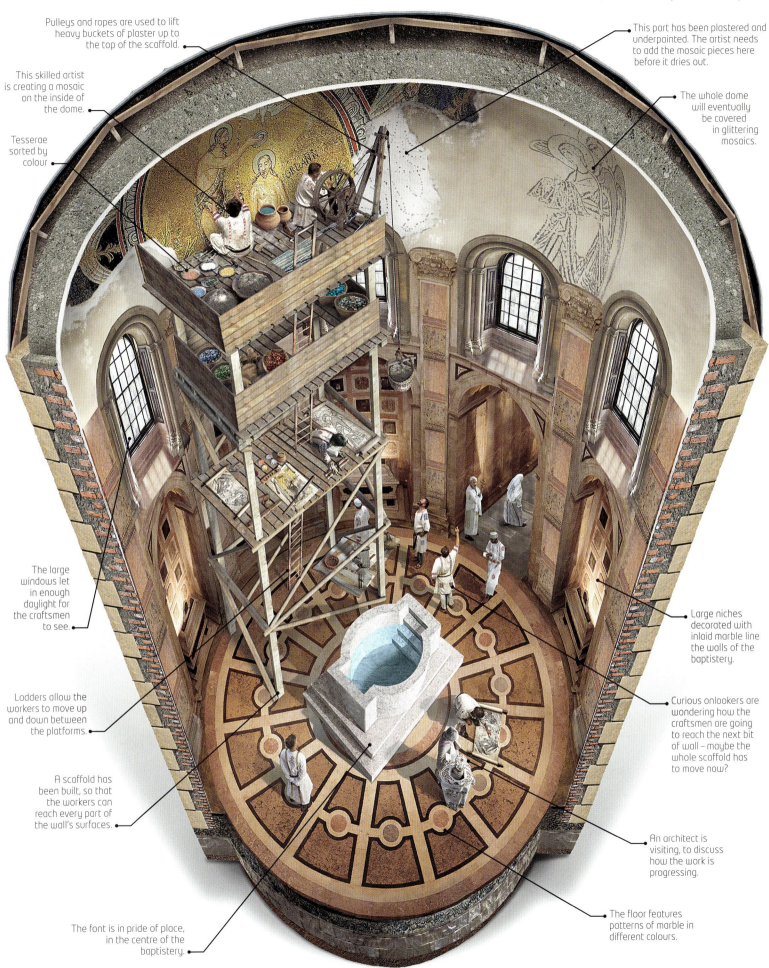

Pulleys and ropes are used to lift heavy buckets of plaster up to the top of the scaffold.

This skilled artist is creating a mosaic on the inside of the dome.

Tesserae sorted by colour

The large windows let in enough daylight for the craftsmen to see.

Ladders allow the workers to move up and down between the platforms.

A scaffold has been built, so that the workers can reach every part of the wall's surfaces.

The font is in pride of place, in the centre of the baptistery.

This part has been plastered and underpainted. The artist needs to add the mosaic pieces here before it dries out.

The whole dome will eventually be covered in glittering mosaics.

Large niches decorated with inlaid marble line the walls of the baptistery.

Curious onlookers are wondering how the craftsmen are going to reach the next bit of wall – maybe the whole scaffold has to move now?

An architect is visiting, to discuss how the work is progressing.

The floor features patterns of marble in different colours.

OLD AND NEW

Hagia Sophia lies in the oldest part of Istanbul, on the peninsula that was once the walled city of Constantinople. To the right of this building are traces of the Byzantine emperor's Great Palace. The wall behind these ruins belongs to the Topkapi Palace, where the Ottoman sultans later lived. Across the waters of the Bosporus Strait, the modern city sprawls in all directions.

JAVANESE TEMPLE

Borobudur is the largest Buddhist temple in the world. Built on Java in the 9th century, it is a four-sided step pyramid with nine levels, rising to a height of 35 m (115 ft). 72 stupas, bell-shaped sculptures containing a statue of the Buddha, decorate the three circular levels at the top of the pyramid. Abandoned at some point after the 11th century, its existence only became internationally known in 1814. It is now a pilgrimage site for Buddhists from around the world.

Island monument
Once at the centre of an ancient kingdom, Borobudur lies on the island of Java, part of the Southeast Asian country of Indonesia. It is surrounded by high mountains and active volcanoes.

Head of the Buddha
Buddhism came to Indonesia from India in the 2nd century CE. The builders of Borobudur placed over 504 statues of the founder of Buddhism, known as the Buddha, on and around the temple.

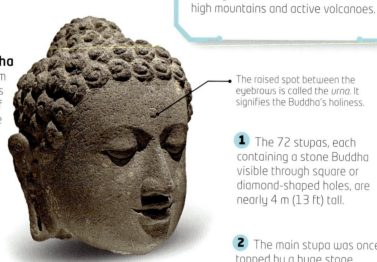

The raised spot between the eyebrows is called the *urna*. It signifies the Buddha's holiness.

1 The 72 stupas, each containing a stone Buddha visible through square or diamond-shaped holes, are nearly 4 m (13 ft) tall.

2 The main stupa was once topped by a huge stone umbrella called a *catra*, which was shattered by lightning.

3 Pilgrims climb to the temple top via the 2,033 stairs and walkways that take them clockwise up to the summit.

Like many Bodhisattvas, Avalokitesvara has several arms.

Holy figure
A Bodhisattva is a human or god who has vowed to help others reach enlightenment, the state of true wisdom all Buddhists ultimately hope to achieve. This statue shows Avalokitesvara, the "Bodhisattva of Compassion". It was made in Java in 700–800 CE, not long before Borobudur was built.

Danger zone
Borobudur sits in the shadow of Mount Merapi, an active volcano. After a series of eruptions, the centre of the Javanese kingdom moved east in around 920 CE, and the temple was later abandoned. In recent years, tarpaulin has been laid out several times to protect the temple from the ash falling during Merapi's eruptions.

Bare stone Borobudur

Borobudur was built by Indonesia's Sailendra dynasty in the 9th century. It was originally clad in white plaster and its friezes brightly painted. When European explorers came across it in the early 19th century, time and weathering had stripped its decorations away, leaving the bare stone that is seen there today. Now cleared and restored, Borobudur is once more a site of pilgrimage – and tourism.

Storytelling sculptures

Borobudur's lower levels bear 1,460 carvings, many depicting the life of the Buddha. Others show the boy Sudhana in search of enlightenment, scenes from heaven and hell, and fairies and animals. This one shows monkeys that, influenced by the Buddha, have become civilized and are eating fruit in a polite manner.

Golden lotus

Famous for its goldsmiths, Java exported exquisit gold jewellery and artifacts all over Asia. This piece is made from finely hammered gold and is in the shape of a lotus – a flower that in Buddhist belief represents purity and enlightenment.

PILGRIMS ARRIVE

It is 900 CE and Buddhist pilgrims are arriving at the great temple of Borobudur on the Indonesian island of Java. They are here for *Vesak*, the annual celebration on the May full moon that marks the life and death of the Buddha. Princes, nobles, men, women, children, and monks will climb the temple, and leave gifts and light candles and lamps in honour of their religion's founder. The most devout will pray and meditate there for hours.

Four-legged transport
Java's elephants were smaller and friendlier, and had bigger ears and longer tails than the Asian elephant. Now extinct on Java, they still exist in Borneo, 1,200 km (746 miles) away.

Hanging lamp
This hanging oil lamp dates from around the time that Borobudur was built. It is in the form of a kinnara, a mythlogical creature that plays music to the gods.

Kinnaras, half-bird, half-human, appear in Hindu and Buddhist beliefs.

The arch is formed by the mouth of Kala, an ancient god said to swallow demons whole.

Lion guard
This grinning stone creature represents a lion. In Buddhist belief, lions mean strength and protection, and there are 32 lions like this one guarding the temple at Borobudur.

These swirling carvings suggest a lion's curly mane.

Symbolic archway
As pilgrims and visitors approach the top of the temple, they must go through ceremonial arches that represent their passing from the world of humans into the world of gods and spirits.

1 **Grand arrival**
VIPs, such as members of Java's ruling Sailendra dynasty, arrive by elephant.

2 **Forest voices**
The surrounding rain forest echoes with the loud calls of monkeys, apes and birds.

3 Holy men
Buddhist monks will lead the ceremonies. They are easy to spot in their orange robes.

4 People of faith
Families and ordinary folk have come from far and wide to praise the Buddha.

5 Way to go
Pilgrims climb the stairs then march clockwise up to Buddha's shrine on top of the temple.

6 Bright building
The white plaster walls and painted friezes stand out against the forest behind.

7 Blaze of glory
The temple's main stupa gleams in the sunlight. It looks magic in moonlight, too.

8 Status symbol
For Buddhists, parasols don't just keep off the sun and rain. They symbolize royalty, too.

GUARDIANS OF THE TEMPLE

The image of Buddha appears all over Borobudur. More than 500 Buddha statues sit cross-legged on the temple's upper levels. Some are visible in the open niches of the middle section, others are enclosed in the 72 stupas at the top. One of these was left uncovered after its original stupa was damaged, allowing visitors a good look.

A PUEBLO GREAT HOUSE

The landscape around Chaco Canyon in the American Southwest is dry, and dotted with towering rock structures. Between the 9th and 13th centuries it was home to a thriving community, who were the ancestors of the Native American people known as Puebloans. They built a number of impressive pueblos (villages) here, known as "great houses", such as Pueblo Bonito.

Canyon country

Pueblo Bonito is located in Chaco Canyon in New Mexico, USA. There are many ancient Puebloan archaeological sites in the area. The region is still home to Pueblo people, as well as the Navajo.

Learning from trees

About a quarter of a million trees were used in the buildings in Pueblo Bonito, and other sites in the canyon. Scientists analyze the wood by studying its tree rings. This tells them the age of the wood, and therefore when buildings were constructed. Other methods can reveal where the trees once grew.

Wooden beams supporting floors and roofs stick out of the walls.

1 Buildings were designed as a series of interconnecting rooms. They were built on more than one level, and people used ladders to move between levels.

2 Communal life took place in the open plaza areas. The round, partly sunken ceremonial rooms that line them are called kivas.

3 This rockfall, which occurred in 1941, damaged many rooms.

Hoarding information

Pack rats hoard all sorts of material in their nests. Pueblo Bonito's ancient middens contain anything from seeds and sticks to pottery and food fragments, preserved by crystallized rat urine. Archaeologists use this material to learn about life in the pueblo.

Modern Pueblo

The descendants of the early Puebloans still live across the Southwest of the USA. This is the traditional Pueblo village of Acoma, built on top of a mesa (flat-topped, steep hill). It has more than 250 houses.

Location of the "Sun dagger" petroglyph (rock carving)

A butte is a tall tower of rock, with steep sides.

Fajada Butte

Landscapes and nature have always been very important to the Pueblo people. Some of the rock formations in Chaco Canyon, such as Fajada Butte, have a spiritual meaning, and are marked with Puebloan carvings.

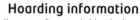
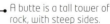

Grandest of the pueblos

Pueblo Bonito is the largest of the many pueblos in Chaco Canyon. Built at the foot of a steep, flat-topped cliff, it has a D-shaped layout, with the buildings laid out around central plazas. Some buildings were four storeys high, and there were up to 600–800 rooms. The site was abandoned in the 13th century. The ruins are now part of the Chaco Culture National Historical Park.

Roofless kiva

Pueblo Bonito's many kivas are round, partly-underground rooms which were used for ceremonies. They originally had wooden roofs, supported by beams. Today, hearths and benches are left open to sun, rain, and snow.

Sun dagger

Some petroglyphs (carvings) at Fajada Butte were made to mark seasonal events. Shafts of sunlight would shine through the rock slabs and fall on the spiral carved behind. Different "dagger" patterns appeared on solstices and equinoxes, depending on the angle of the sunbeams hitting the rock.

Sun's position at summer solstice

Rock face

Slabs placed against the rock, with spaces allowing sunlight to shine onto the rock face.

At the summer solstice, the "sun dagger" produced by sunbeams falls in the centre of the spiral.

Spiral carved into the rock face

PUEBLO LIFE

It is the 11th century, and Pueblo Bonito is bustling with activity. Its many rooms are used for living in, storage, or even as burial chambers, but much of its daily life takes place outside. Some Puebloans are working to repair and extend the pueblo. Others are busy cooking, crafting, and trading goods.

This is the oldest part of the pueblo

Pueblo entrance   Great kiva

Great house

Pueblo Bonito was built upon and expanded over several centuries. By this time, its buildings and kivas centred around two large open plazas. There was only one entrance, and no doors or large windows along the outer walls.

Turquoise trade

The mineral turquoise was prized for its beautiful blue-green colour. It was mined and traded over a vast network. Pueblo Bonito was a key centre both for trading and for turning turquoise into jewellery and ceremonial objects.

Scarlet macaws

These birds were imported from Mexico, far to the south of Chaco Canyon. They were kept indoors, but not as pets – their bones and brightly-coloured feathers were used in rituals and ceremonies.

Pueblo pottery

Black-and-white pottery, such as this pitcher, was produced in Pueblo Bonito. Bowls, ladles, and beakers were also made. Some vessels found here show traces of cocoa. Prepared with beans from the cacao tree, this was a ceremonial drink for Puebloans.

1 Roof repair
Skilled builders are laying out a new kiva roof, using sturdy wood beams for support.

2 Cooking time
It's hot work cooking corn breads over an open fire, but they smell delicious.

3 Corn flour
A stone slab known as a *metate* is used to grind corn (maize) down into flour.

4 Time to trade
This trader has all sorts of goods for sale, including shells and turquoise beads.

5 Heavy load
It takes three men to carry this long, heavy pine tree trunk to the kiva building site.

6 Sandal-making
This woman weaves a new pair of sandals from the tough fibres of a yucca plant.

7 Catch it!
A macaw has escaped! This man is desperately trying to recapture the rare and valuable bird.

8 Good boy
There are a number of dogs at Pueblo Bonito. They live with and alongside the people.

ANCIENT CARVINGS
The area around Pueblo Bonito and the other Pueblo great houses in Chaco Canyon contains many ancient petroglyphs – images carved into the rocks. Some depict patterns, human figures, and animals, such as bighorn sheep, while others mark astronomical observations.

THE SULTAN'S PALACE

High on a cliff above the city of Granada in Spain stands a grand palace complex, known as the Alhambra, built from glowing red sandstone. This was once the seat of power for the Kingdom of Granada, a realm in southern Spain that was ruled over by Muslim sultans. The Alhambra is made up of a series of interconnecting buildings, open courtyards, and peaceful gardens, all featuring beautiful and complex decorations.

The sunny south
The Alhambra is in a part of Spain called Andalucia. The area is hot and dry, so buildings like the Alhambra were designed to allow cool air to circulate.

Palace with a view
The Alhambra was built above Granada, which gave it a clear view across the surrounding area. It was built on the site of an old military fortress by Muhammad I, the first ruler of the Kingdom of Granada. In the 18th century, the palace was abandoned. In the following centuries, work to restore the palace began, and it is now a National Monument of Spain.

1

City and state
The city of Granada was capital of the Kingdom of Granada. This was the last independent Muslim state in Europe when it was invaded by the Christian Kingdom of Castile in 1492.

This is the Kingdom of Granada's coat of arms. The writing celebrates the greatness of Allah (god).

1 The palace is named after the colour of its stone – *al-hamra* means "the red" in Arabic.

This gold filigree necklace was made in Granada in the 14th century.

Skilled craftspeople
Medieval Granada was a wealthy city, and attracted many skilled craftspeople, including jewellers. The gold they used for some of their finest work came from Africa, by trade routes that crossed the Sahara Desert.

The Palace of the Lions is centred around a courtyard that features a fountain held up by stone lions.

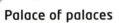

Palace of palaces
There were several palaces in the Alhambra. The Palace of the Lions was probably the royal family's private home. The Mexuar Palace was used for state business, and the Comares was the sultan's official residence.

A Muslim dynasty
This ceiling painting shows ten sultans of the Nasrid dynasty, which ruled the Kingdom of Granada. The eighth sultan, Muhammad V, built the Palace of the Lions.

2 The Hall of the Ambassadors was a reception space, where the ruler would greet important visitors.

3 The Alcazaba is the remains of the original fortress at the Alhambra.

Co-operative art
Muhammad V was Muslim, but he was close to King Pedro I of Castile, who was Christian. This is reflected in the art of the Alhambra which has both Christian and Muslim features. This ceiling painting depicts a hunting scene, and two ladies talking by the fountain.

1 Ibn Zamrak
The poet Ibn Zamrak reads a poem that he has written to celebrate the occasion.

2 Four streams
The fountain's waters run into four streams, which represent the four rivers of Paradise.

3 Twelve lions
Water streams from the carefully carved mouths of the twelve marble lions.

4 Cool fountain
The trickling water adds a cooling effect to the courtyard bathed in hot Andalucian sunlight.

5 Columns
The courtyard columns are carved like palm trees around an oasis in the desert.

6 Four wives
The sultan's wives watch the proceedings, but they don't socialize with his guests.

A NEW FOUNTAIN

Sultan Muhammad V has worked on making the Alhambra even more splendid. So far, one of his most spectacular commissions is the elaborate Lion Fountain, which has just been installed in a courtyard in the Palace of the Lions. Muhammad has gathered his family and courtiers to see his impressive new fountain and to listen to the sound of gently flowing water that fills the air around them.

Splendid ceramics
Luxurious furnishings and finely crafted items such as this vase would have been on display at the Alhambra. Lustreware ceramics glistened with an iridescent sheen. They were made especially for royalty.

Weightless vaults
The delicate honeycomb patterns on the Alhambra's vaulted ceilings make them appear weightless, as if made from lace. Known as *muqarnas*, they were created by Islamic artisans.

The Lion Fountain
This fountain was a masterpiece of medieval plumbing. The water was pumped and drained very precisely, so that the fountain never overflowed.

Skilled in silk
As the last Muslim kingdom left on the Iberian Peninsula, Granada provided refuge to many skilled craftspeople of that faith. The city became famous for the luxury goods it produced, including intricately woven silk, such as this rich, red carpet.

7 Can I touch?
One of the sultan's sons wants to have a closer look at the lions but is told to behave.

8 The Sultan
Muhammad V listens to the poem with his advisers, who admire the new fountain.

DAZZLING DECOR

Set around the courtyards of the Palace of the Lions are rooms with large, arched openings, from which people could admire the plants and fountains while staying in the shade. This room, known as the Mirador de Daraxa, is elaborately decorated with colourful tilework and intricately carved structures called *muqarnas*.

GREAT STONE CITY

Great Zimbabwe was once the capital of the wealthy Kingdom of Zimbabwe. Its monumental stone walls were built between the 11th and 16th centuries, by Bantu-speaking ancestors of the Shona people who live in the area today.

Historic kingdom
Great Zimbabwe lies in the country of Zimbabwe. The land it controlled extended across modern-day Zimbabwe, Zambia, Mozambique, and South Africa.

Colossal structures
The capital's Great Enclosure was built on a massive scale. The tower and walls of this complex are many times taller than a person – the tower is 10 m (33 ft) high.

1 The Hill Complex is the oldest part of this site. It was once the home of the king, before the seat of power moved to the Great Enclosure.

This is a cast of a soapstone dish found at Great Zimbabwe, featuring a crocodile.

Search for clues
When Great Zimbabwe was excavated by European visitors in the late 19th century, many artefacts were removed to museums without much care or documentation. As a result, insight into their significance was lost. Objects found here today, from gold bracelets and ceramic pieces to tools used for farming and metal smelting, help reveal how people here lived and what they produced.

Soapstone bird
Eight carved soapstone birds have been found at Great Zimbabwe. They were placed on walls and monoliths, and are believed to have been symbols of the kings, gods, or ancestors.

Updated digs
Modern archaeologists have re-examined Great Zimbabwe's ruins, including "everyday" areas, such as kitchens (seen here). Research and local knowledge have replaced colonial interpretations, which were based on false – and racist – ideas.

Once bustling city
Set on a fertile plain, Great Zimbabwe was once rich and prosperous. There was good grazing for cattle, which were a key marker of wealth, and skilled craftspeople produced goods for local use as well as for trade. The city was surrounded by more than 4,000 mines, supplying a lot of the gold used in faraway countries. But in around 1550, for reasons not fully known, its inhabitants moved north, to Mutapa, and it fell into ruin.

2 The Valley Complex was home to farmers, craftspeople, and merchants. They lived in mud houses with thatched roofs, inside enclosures.

3 The Great Enclosure was a royal fortress. Its walls encircled living quarters and a solid conical tower whose function is not known.

Golden kingdoms
The mining and trading of gold made Great Zimbabwe, and other kingdoms in the region, rich. This gold rhinoceros was made in the kingdom of Mapungubwe, in the 13th century.

Mighty walls
Great Zimbabwe's walls were carefully designed and built to stand firm without the use of mortar between the stones. Some sections have stones placed in decorative patterns.

1 Hill to climb
Some priests and their helpers are heading to the ceremonial site inside the Hill Complex.

2 Daily work
A blacksmith is at work in this small enclosure. He is producing useful tools made from iron.

3 Wise council
Elders are gathering to discuss important matters in the shade of the milkwood tree.

4 Good trade
This caravan is going back to east Africa's Swahili coast, loaded with gold and ivory.

5 Play fight
Younger members of the royal family are testing their speed and strength in the yard.

6 Cash cows
Herders keep a close eye on the cattle they are tending – cows are extremely valuable.

A BUSY DAY

It is early morning, but most of the 20,000 people who live in Great Zimbabwe are already up and about. There is cattle to look after, iron and precious metals to mine and process, and food to harvest and prepare. But the city is extra lively today as the Swahili merchants are departing, loaded with goods. The king and his people will celebrate another successful trade.

Trade networks

Great Zimbabwe was well placed to grow rich. It traded with other nearby kingdoms, and with the Swahili states on Africa's east coast. These states then traded internationally, with China and countries that were positioned around the Indian Ocean. Foreign goods, such as this delicate Chinese teapot, often found their way to Great Zimbabwe.

This Chinese jade teapot was found during excavations at Great Zimbabwe.

Cowrie currency

Cowrie shells were used as a form of currency in Great Zimbabwe as well as in other kingdoms in the region, and along the global trade routes. Beautiful as well as valuable, the shells could be made into jewellery or other ornaments, too.

Gold-ringed cowries were the species most commonly used in the region.

This is a modern Zimbabwean cow.

A female figure carved from soapstone

The women of Great Zimbabwe

Women played key roles in the economy and agriculture of Great Zimbabwe. They were involved in weaving and mining, and might have also traded. Women could wield power, too – queens were very influential.

Treasured cattle

Cows have been grazing on the Zimbabwe Plateau since it was first settled. Cattle were very valuable. They were the main indicator of a king's wealth, and could be traded for gold.

7 **Local wildlife**
Wild animals live close to the city. Zebras, giraffes, and rhinos graze near the cattle.

8 **Revered bird**
A bateleur eagle, the inspiration for the city's soapstone bird statues, soars in the sky above.

HIGH ON THE HILL

Perched on a high summit, Great Zimbabwe's Hill Complex overlooks the Valley Complex and the Great Enclosure far below. It is the oldest part of the site, occupied from the 9th century. Later, when the king moved down into the Great Enclosure, it is thought to have been used for royal ceremonies and other rituals. Seven of the eight famous soapstone bird statues were found here.

FALLEN CASTLE

Perched on a steep hillside, and commanding a stretch of the Neckar River, the ruins of Heidelberg Castle in Germany are steeped in history. First built as a fortified home for the rulers of the region, the castle was rebuilt as a palace during the Renaissance, when style was considered more important than defence. Fires caused by lightning strikes have since burned it down twice, and it has been blown up on two separate occasions. Although a ruin today, it stands as a reminder of the city's past glories.

Strategic location
Heidelberg Castle sits 91 m (300 ft) above the Neckar River in southwest Germany. It protects the medieval city of Heidelberg in the valley below.

Jigsaw castle
Construction on Heidelberg Castle began in the early 1200s and continued, off and on, for another 400 years. That is why each one of its buildings looks so different from the others, even though they are joined together. They were all built in the local sandstone that makes the castle "glow" pink in certain lights – especially summer and autumn sunsets.

Lone fountain
The palace was once famous for its gardens. Today, only the fountain known as "Father Rhine" gives a hint of their splendour, and the water mechanics admired by the court.

The Powder Tower
Known as the *Pulverturm* in German, this is where the castle's gunpowder supplies were stored. It exploded spectacularly in 1689, completely splitting in half.

1 The Powder Tower

2 The Ottheinrich Building

3 The eight-sided Bell Tower, built in the 15th century, was originally a gun tower with cannons on every floor.

4 The Friedrich Building was the rulers' main living quarters. On its right is the ruined "English Building", once built by Frederick V for his wife, Elizabeth Stuart, daughter of King James I of England.

5 The walls of the *Dicker Turm* ("fat tower") were 7 m (22 ft) thick. Today, the ruin hosts performances.

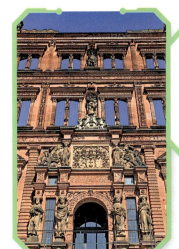

Surviving lightning
The castle's Ottheinrich Building was hit by a lightning strike in 1714. The richly-decorated façade, or front, of the building survived but behind it, only the ground floor remains.

Gigantic barrel
The castle's wine cellar is home to what is said to be the world's largest wine barrel, the Heidelberg Tun ("tun" is an old word for barrel). It was made in 1751 and can hold 221,726 litres (48,773 gallons).

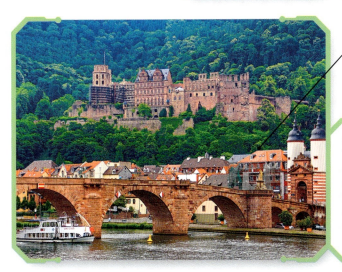

The city of Heidelberg has been here as long as the castle. It has one of Europe's oldest universities.

Commanding view
The castle sits high above the Neckar, a tributary to the Rhine, one of Europe's main rivers. From here, the rulers would have had a good overview of approaching enemies, but it didn't help when the French attacked in the 17th century.

BLASTED APART!

It is 6 September 1689, and soldiers of the French army are ending their occupation of Heidelberg. Capital of the German state known as the Palatinate, the city had been occupied during a wider European war. As the French retreat, and to weaken the Palatinate's defences against any future attack, they blow up Heidelberg's castle with 12 tonnes (27,000 lb) of explosives. If they cannot have it, then no one else will!

Flintlocks were beautifully carved and ornamented with silver.

Tricky weapon
The flintlock pistols used at this time were highly decorative, but difficult to use. They were heavy, not very accurate, and it took at least 20 seconds to reload one after it had fired its single ball of shot.

Double trouble
Heidelberg suffered multiple attacks in the 17th century. As well as the attack depicted in this 1689 engraving, the French attacked again four years later, further damaging the castle.

French soldiers ride through the burning town of Heidelberg as the people beg for mercy.

Castle defences
By the 17th century, Heidelberg Castle was more of a palace than a military stronghold. But it was still well defended, with thick, high walls, a fortified gatehouse, and, overlooking the city and river, cannons that could keep at bay enemy troops attacking up the hill.

Difficult times
The population of Heidelberg had experienced several attacks and occupations by different armies during this time of wars in Europe. In 1689, part of their town was burned down, too.

Cannons have handles positioned at their centre of gravity, so that it is easier to lift and move them.

1 **The big bang!**
The castle's gunpowder supplies blow up, causing the biggest explosion of the night.

2 **Perfect timing**
38 mines laid around the castle go off at once. This one blasts the main courtyard.

3 No exit
The heat and smoke near the main gateway make it difficult for anyone to escape.

4 Ding dong gone
The whole top of the octagonal Bell Tower is blown clean off, taking the bell inside with it!

5 Smoke damage
Thick smoke blackens furniture and works of art on the top floors of the Friedrich Building.

6 Fierce fire
The blaze in the "English Building" will leave just the façade standing at the end.

7 Job done
French troops watch as the fires they have lit take hold and begin to ravage the castle.

8 The horror!
Townsfolk from Heidelberg watch in disbelief as their beloved castle burns.

GRAND GARDENS
An ambitious gardening project had begun at Heidelberg Castle in 1616. Terraces were built on the steep slope, filled with geometrical plant beds as well as hidden grottoes and mechanized moving statues. Sadly, due to the outbreak of wars and conflicts, the famous Palatine Gardens were never fully finished, and soon fell into ruin.

CONFUCIAN ACADEMY

Gently rolling hills, woodland, and flowing rivers surround the ancient academy of Dosan Seowon in South Korea. This peaceful place was founded in the 16th century, 2,000 years after the death of the Chinese philosopher Confucius, whose teachings it was established to study. In a tradition continuing for hundreds of years, learned scholars taught their students the Confucian ideals of fairness, respect, ethics, morality, and education.

Confucian centre
Dosan Seowon sits on the banks of Nakdonggang, South Korea's longest river. It was one of a number of academies in the region, which was known for producing famous scholars.

Plum blossom, Yi Hwang's favourite flower, decorates this modern Korean banknote.

Royal seals like this one, shaped like a turtle, was used by Joseon kings to sign documents.

Scholarly kings
The Joseon dynasty ruled Korea for more than 500 years. Seonjo, who was king when Dosan Seowon was founded, became known for encouraging Confucianism – a philosophy that emphasized fairness and education.

Yi Hwang

Yi Hwang
A famous Confucian scholar, Yi Hwang, founded the first school in this location in 1560. This small school had two purposes: to teach its students and to hold memorial rites to honour ancient Confucian philosophers.

The cranes shown in this Joseon painting are a symbol of respect for parents and ancestors, but also of "aloof" scholars.

Observing nature
When scholars and students were not teaching or studying, they would go walking, in order to contemplate rocks, trees, and rivers. Understanding and being respectful of nature played an important part in Confucian philosophy.

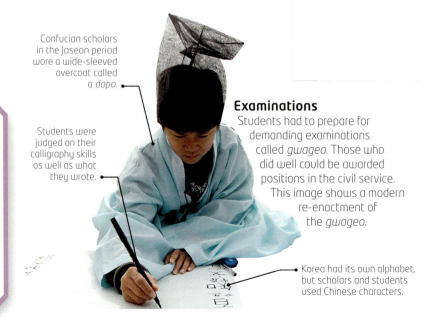

Confucian scholars in the Joseon period wore a wide-sleeved overcoat called a dopo.

Students were judged on their calligraphy skills as well as what they wrote.

Examinations
Students had to prepare for demanding examinations called gwageo. Those who did well could be awarded positions in the civil service. This image shows a modern re-enactment of the gwageo.

Korea had its own alphabet, but scholars and students used Chinese characters.

Home of learning
When Yi Hwang founded his school, he built only one room, in which he both slept and taught his students. After Yi Hwang's death in 1570, an academy was founded in his honour, and many more buildings were added. They included dormitories for the students, a shrine, libraries, and a publishing house. Today, Dosan Seowon is open for visitors and has a museum. It still hosts commemorative ceremonies.

1 This small, enclosed building is Yi Hwang's original school. He also designed a garden here, with a pond and many different plants.

2 The libraries contained more than 5,000 books. They were originally built at ground level, but later raised up on stilts, to help keep the books dry.

3 The academy's lecture hall is where main lessons took place.

Roof detail
Traditional Korean buildings have roofs covered in interlocking clay tiles. The round end tile of each row is decorated with intricate patterns and symbols, which can feature plants, animals, or Chinese characters.

陶山書院

1 High hat
Tall, wide-brimmed hats, called *kat*, were worn by the social elite, including scholars.

2 Hurry up!
These students need to hurry – being late for class would be very disrespectful.

3 Lecture hall
The main part of the lecture hall is open. The enclosed section is the principal's living room.

4 Pride of place
This is the name of the academy. It was written by master calligrapher Han Seok-bong.

5 Keen students
Most of the students are already in the lecture hall. They sit in neat rows.

6 Master scholar
This teacher is very strict but he enjoys passing on his vast knowledge.

TIME FOR CLASS

It is early September 1580. The myrtle trees of Dosan Seowon are still in bloom. Inside the academy, the students are studying hard. A class led by a greatly respected master scholar is just beginning in the lecture hall. After class, the pupils will practise their debating skills, and then listen to lectures about good and bad ways of life, and responsibility. Then they might do some calligraphy, before taking a walk down the path to the river.

Woodblock
Books were printed using carved woodblocks, which were coated in ink, then pressed onto paper made from the bark of mulberry trees. The blocks were then stored away in the publishing house.

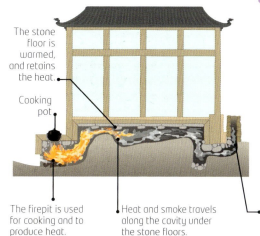

Four friends
Calligraphy is writing, but it is also an art form. The four essentials that are needed to create calligraphy are known as the "Four Friends". They are a brush, ink, inkstone, and paper.

The stone floor is warmed, and retains the heat.

Cooking pot

Underfloor heating
People in Korea traditionally sat and slept on their floor. To make this more comfortable, they used an underfloor heating system, known as *ondol*. The enclosed part of the lecture hall at Dosan Seowon had *ondol* heating.

The firepit is used for cooking and to produce heat.

Heat and smoke travels along the cavity under the stone floors.

The chimney creates draft, allowing the smoke to escape.

7 Admiring nature
Guest scholars marvel at the beauty of the myrtle tree, perhaps composing poems about it.

8 Librarian
The librarian is taking some books of classic Confucian texts back to the library.

Fermented foods
Students ate rice and fermented pickles such as kimchi, made from cabbage, chilli, and garlic. Pickles and spicy pastes were stored in huge clay pots kept in one of the courtyards.

A DANCING SCHOLAR

The scholars of Dosan Seowon were highly respected for their learning. However, they were made fun of in traditional dance performances. The Hahoe mask dance is still performed today, in a village not far from the academy. The wooden mask with bulging eyes worn by this dancer shows he is playing the role of a scholar.

ROYAL PALACE

Not far from Paris, in what was once the French countryside, sits Versailles, one of the most opulent palaces the world has ever seen. In the 17th century, over a period of more than 40 years, the King of France, Louis XIV, converted an old royal hunting lodge into a vast palace. Here, he could dazzle his friends and enemies alike with lavish parties and receptions. In 1682, it also became his official seat of government. Added to by his successors, the palace is as impressive today.

Large parts of the buildings are gilded (covered in a thin layer of gold leaf).

Royal powerbase

Versailles is located just outside Paris, in northern France. Nobles from across the country were summoned to the palace, where the king could keep an eye on them and assert his power.

The Sun King

Louis XIV believed himself to be at the centre of the universe, an absolute monarch around whom everything revolved, with a divine right to rule his people. He aimed to impress foreign powers and his own people with displays of his wealth and status. He supported many artists, who were paid to depict Louis as a magnificent golden "Sun King".

This image shows Louis XIV dressed as Apollo, the ancient Greek god of the Sun, for a ballet in 1653.

Grand designs

Louis spared no expense in his plans to expand Versailles. He invited the most famous architects and gardeners to design the palace's new sections, the vast formal gardens, and 50 different fountains.

Perfume was placed in the bowl and heated up with a spirit lamp.

The perfumed court

The court at Versailles was splendid, but it would have also been quite smelly – there were no toilets and people took baths very rarely, as water was thought to spread disease. To hide the smell, people used huge quantities of strongly-scented perfumes. Perfume burners allowed the scent to spread through the rooms.

Perfume burners remained popular. This one was bought for Queen Marie Antoinette, in the late 18th century.

The Palace of Versailles has more than 2,000 windows. The lead dividing their panes was originally gilded.

The King's Chamber is where Louis XIV's official getting-up ceremony, the *lever*, took place.

Fit for a king

Louis XIV employed several architects to improve and expand Versailles, transforming it into a magnificent palace. Over the years, wings were added, façades were altered, and decorative features appeared and disappeared. The Marble Courtyard, seen here, was once enclosed by a colonnade, but it was taken down and the sumptuous King's Chamber added at the back, crowned by a clock.

Golden balconies overlook the Royal Courtyard, the space in front of the smaller Marble Courtyard.

Wonderful wigs

This waxwork shows Louis XIV in his later life. As the king reached middle age, his hair began to fall out. To hide his baldness, Louis wore flowing wigs, which became court fashion.

The Hall of Mirrors

One of the most famous rooms at Versailles is the Hall of Mirrors. It is lined with 357 mirrors, which were rare and difficult to produce in the 17th century.

AN EVENING BALL

The Sun is setting. The Palace of Versailles, lit by glimmering lights, is ready to welcome several thousand guests for one of Louis XIV's famous balls. Carriages line up in front of the palace and their occupants wait to descend, talking excitedly about the night ahead. There will be music, dancing, and intrigues - may the spectacle begin!

1 Carriage queue
A long line of carriages is waiting. Their occupants are keen to disembark.

2 Excited guest
This young lady has never been to a royal ball before. She wonders if she'll meet the king.

3 Changing tastes
The colonnade, dividing the two courtyards, was taken down during later renovations.

4 Late night lights
Oil lamps and chandeliers light up the grand rooms. Servants will keep them burning all night.

5 Royal Guard
This man is one of Louis' own guards, stationed around the palace to protect their king.

6 Welcome, milady
A courtier greets the guests, making sure to address them with the right name and title.

7 Fancy feathers
Ostrich feathers add style to the fashionable men's hats known as tricorns.

8 Exclusive fashion
Like all nobles coming to the ball, this couple have spent a fortune on their outfits.

9 Etiquette rules
Status matters hugely – this couple has to wait for higher-ranking nobles to enter first.

10 Potted trees
Citrus trees line the inner courtyard. They have been brought all the way from Italy.

11 Chimneys
The palace needs lots of chimneys for the 1,200 fireplaces that keep it warm.

TRAVELLING IN STYLE

A noble's carriage is a work of art – a highly-decorated, gilded status symbol, which also just happens to be a fine mode of transport. The rich and famous use their carriages to highlight their wealth and impeccable fashion sense. This example has just arrived at one of Louis XIV's balls – it is the very best its occupants can afford, and they're hoping everyone notices it!

The carriage is decorated with gilded wood carvings. It is just as fancy inside.

Courtly glamour

This portrait shows the famous beauty Hortense Mancini modelling the latest fashions and the "hurlyburly" hairstyle. Fashion was very important to Louis XIV and his court and strict rules governed what people could wear.

The coat of arms lets people know whose carriage this is – all noble families have their own.

An unusually large pink diamond, this was left to the French king by Cardinal Mazarin. It is known as the Grand Mazarin diamond.

Diamond fever

Louis XIV loved gemstones, and diamonds in particular. As well as jewellery, he wore clothes encrusted with diamonds, and had pictures of himself framed with them. Everyone else at court had to copy the king – records mention nobles heavily weighed down with gems.

This diamond was set into the French crown and worn by a series of French rulers.

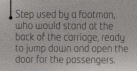

Step used by a footman, who would stand at the back of the carriage, ready to jump down and open the door for the passengers.

Big wooden wheels make for a bumpy ride when rolling across uneven ground. The carriage's suspension, made from leather straps, doesn't help much.

Royal road trip

Fine carriages weren't just used at court. This painting shows Queen Maria Theresa and her ladies approaching Arras during one of Louis' campaigns, the king following on a white horse.

State-of-the-art sliding windows allow the passengers to take a look outside.

The price of fashion

Fashionable shoes were uncomfortable, and often had high heels. They were also very expensive, which meant people didn't want to get them dirty. This made the idea of taking carriage or sedan chair rides to cross Versailles' vast grounds extremely appealing.

Two horses pull this carriage, but some were pulled by up to six animals.

PALATIAL STABLES

Horses were the main mode of transport at Versailles, so Louis built two matching, semi-circular stables outside the palace gates. These ornate buildings, seen at the top of this painting, had stalls to house up to 600 horses.

King's symbol

Symbols appear all over Versailles – including on carriages, and even on horses. This part of a horse's harness has the king's own symbol, featuring the Ancient Greek Sun god, Apollo.

THE MORNING ROUTINE

The king's day follows a strict timetable. Even his daily routines are ceremonial, and watched by an audience. Louis XIV has been awake for a while, and the first ceremony of the day is complete. Now it's time for the *lever* – the grand getting-up ceremony. To watch the king get dressed and eat breakfast is a great honour, and entrance to this spectacle is strictly controlled.

1 The Usher of the King's Room has a list of the attendees planned for today. He makes sure no-one else is allowed in.

2 One of the king's loyal guards is waiting for his turn to speak to the king. He is hoping to get a position for his younger brother.

The king's architect
People working on projects for the king could have a private audience with him at the *lever*. Among them was Louis' architect, Jules Hardouin-Mansart, who designed some of the most famous buildings and features of Versailles.

This coin bears the face of Louis XIV. It was named the *Louis d'or* (golden Louis) after the king.

Paying for the privilege
Although only the most favoured family members, nobles, and servants had access to the *lever* ceremony, those without an invitation could buy their way in, at a price.

Decorations in brass and red tortoiseshell cover the surface of the table.

5 Among the favoured attendees is the king's eldest son, Louis, Le Grand Dauphin.

6 Louis' chief architect, Jules Hardouin-Mansart, is waiting to show the king plans for a new folly.

Fine furnishings
Louis XIV had many pieces of furniture made for his apartments, to suit his expensive tastes. They were often decorated with images of the French crown, Louis' monogram, or even images of the king himself. This writing table features Louis' monogram on its surface.

7 This grand bishop, Monseigneur Bossuet, is Louis' court preacher, and was also the tutor of his son, Le Grand Dauphin.

3 Louis' bedroom is richly decorated, and filled with beautiful furniture and objects such as this chandelier.

4 The king's grand bed is surrounded by thick curtains, to keep out draughts. Sometimes he will give an audience from the warmth of his bed.

Brilliant bed

Louis XIV remodelled his official bedroom in 1701. The walls and curtains around his bed were covered with red, gold, and silver brocade. Above the bed is a gilded carved decoration of France (shown as a woman) watching over the king's sleep. He died in this bed in 1715, after a week of illness, at the age of 76.

Royal breakfast

Part of the *lever* was watching Louis eat breakfast. His breakfast was fairly simple – it might have been soup, bread dipped in wine, or slices of cold meat.

The king's soup was served in a silver tureen.

Dressing the king

Louis XIV was dressed with the help of a number of servants. His clothes were put on in a particular order, starting with the undergarments and ending with a knee-length coat called a *justaucorps*.

Justaucorps had long sleeves and buttons running all the way along the front.

A balustrade separates the king from petitioners and courtiers.

8 The Officers of the Royal Wardrobe are lined up next to the king, waiting to pass him pieces of clothing.

9 Louis XIV is at the centre of the action. He is getting dressed while listening to petitions from his guests.

10 This servant is ready and waiting with the king's breakfast.

A NIGHT TO REMEMBER

Louis XIV is throwing a party, and it's going to be spectacular. The gardens at his new palace have just been redesigned, and Louis is keen to show them off – guests will admire their exquisite geometry. On top of this, the king has organized the premiere of a new play, a grand feast, and a ball. Finally, the evening will end with a firework display, designed to highlight the grandeur of the new palace.

1 The palace is not yet finished, so there is not enough room inside for all of Louis' guests to stay. Soon, however, the king will demand that his courtiers move in, and up to 10,000 people will live and work here.

Stunning statues
Louis XIV wanted fine statues and sculpted fountains placed throughout his gardens, and kept commissioning new ones. Here the king and his courtiers admire a new statue, *Milo of Croton* by the sculptor Pierre Puget.

Louis XIV, surrounded by his favourite courtiers

ROYAL GUARDS

Throughout the palace and its grounds, guests would spot men in the striking blue uniform of Louis' Royal Guards. The 3,000 guardsmen were responsible for protecting the king and could confiscate the weapons of anyone they deemed a threat.

2 Statues of Greek gods and goddesses line the walkways. Their white marble bodies glimmer in the dusk.

3 Some nobles have ventured out on foot to explore the illuminated paths, and perhaps have a secret conversation.

4 The passenger in this sedan chair regrets not taking his carriage – the carriers almost dropped him at the entrance.

Fireworks blaze into the sky above the palace.

The central section shown here is only a tiny part of the gardens, which take up the space of nearly a thousand football pitches.

9 Hidden among these trees are specially designed, sheltered groves with fountains, where the king loves to walk.

Travelling chair

Nobles often used sedan chairs (seats carried by two men – one at the front and one at the back) to spare them from having to walk around the extensive gardens at Versailles.

Sailing ships decorate this sedan chair dating from slightly after the reign of Louis XIV.

Brackets at each corner for the two poles that the carriers used to lift and keep the chair off the ground.

These paper cards were printed with handcarved woodcuts.

Playing cards

Many French nobles played card games for entertainment, and the king himself was a big player. Gambling was common at the palace, and people could lose huge sums and even their entire fortunes at the gaming tables.

5 A temporary marquee has been built to shelter the king and his guests while they watch the spectacular fireworks.

6 Carriage horses have to be calm and patient animals, not easily startled by fireworks or other noise.

7 An army of gardeners have spent hours trimming the plants into the precise patterns of the formal gardens.

8 This fountain shows the young god Apollo, with his sister Diana and his mother Latona, in a scene from a Greek myth.

VISITING VERSAILLES

Ambassadors from all over the world came to visit Louis XIV at Versailles, including this delegation from Siam (Thailand). They brought him expensive and exotic gifts, and were given presents by him in turn. Many of the gifts Louis gave to diplomats featured his symbols or even himself, often in his role as the "Sun King".

GIGANTIC PALACE

When China's Yongle Emperor decided to move his capital from Nanjing to Beijing in the early 1400s, he built for himself a huge walled palace complex. His palace became known as the Forbidden City because commoners were not allowed to set foot inside it without permission. For 600 years the complex has resisted fires, wars, rebellions, and revolutions. It still stands as an almost perfectly preserved monument to China's two great, late imperial dynasties, the Ming and the Qing.

City within a city
The Forbidden City is located in China's capital, Beijing. It lies in the historical area of the city, which is surrounded by the towerblocks of modern Beijing.

The Forbidden City today
The Forbidden City covers an area of 720,000 sq m (7.75 million sq ft), about the size of 100 football pitches. Around one million labourers constructed the complex's 980 buildings, which include more than 90 small palaces and courtyards, and 8,728 rooms. Twenty-four Chinese emperors lived there between 1420 and 1912, when a revolution ended the empire. These days, visitors fill its renovated halls.

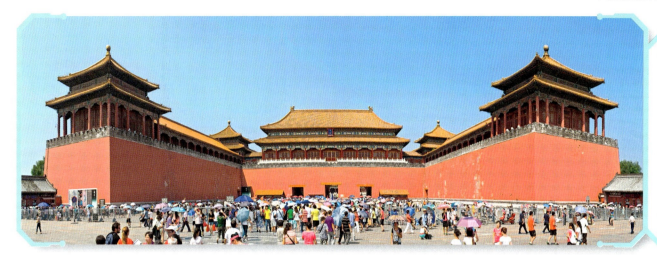

Meridian Gate
The main way into the Forbidden City was through the southern Meridian Gate. This imposing entrance towers to 37.95 m (124.5 ft) at its highest point. Except on a few special occasions, only the emperor could use the middle portal.

Corner towers
Each of the Forbidden City's four corners was overlooked by watch towers. But these were not what they seemed: they were hollow inside. There was not even a floor between each level, as they were built to look good rather than being used for defence.

Zhu Di, the fourth son of the first Ming emperor, seized power in a civil war. He chose the reign-name Yongle, meaning "perpetual happiness".

1 The main palaces are arranged in a straight, central line, running south to north, with the Hall of Supreme Harmony in the middle.

2 The northern entrance is the Gate of Divine Might. This was the back entrance to the city, used by staff and servants.

3 The Forbidden City is surrounded on all four sides by brick walls 8 m (26 ft) high.

The incense burners were used for important events and filled with wild honey, cloves, and aloe vera that perfumed the air.

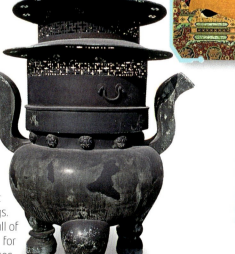

Yongle Emperor
Work on the Forbidden City began in 1406, under the reign of Yongle, the third emperor of the Ming Dynasty. It was designed by the architect Kuai Xiang and took 14 years to build.

Incense burner
Up to 4 m (12 ft) tall, decorated bronze *ding* (incense burners) sat outside the palace's main buildings. There were 18 at the Hall of Surpreme Harmony alone, one for each of China's provinces.

A SPECIAL DAY

It is 26 February 1889. China's new empress-to-be Jinfeng arrives at the Hall of Supreme Harmony in the heart of Beijing's Forbidden City. Her wedding ceremony to the Guangxu Emperor is about to begin.

1 Powerful beasts
Gilded bronze lions stand as symbols of the power and majesty of the emperor.

2 Fire guards
The Chinese believe the *chiwen*, or dragons, at the corners of the roof can drive away fire.

3 Sweet perfume
A scent of sandalwood from the three-legged, pot-bellied *ding* incense burners fill the air.

4 Drumming up support
Large buffalo-skin drums called *tanggu* will be struck at key moments in the ceremony.

5 Colour coded
The blue-green and yellow in the canopy represent harmony, long life, and imperial power.

6 Name plate
The characters on the blue plaque spell out the words "Hall of Supreme Harmony".

7 Precious passenger
Jinfeng sits hidden inside the golden palanquin, waiting for the ceremony to begin.

8 Red carpet treatment
A red carpet marks Jinfeng's route to the ceremony. Red is a symbol of luck and celebration.

9 Qing dynasty hair
All men had the same hairstyle: shaved at the front with a long, plaited pony tail at the back.

10 Broad shoulders
Sixteen guards have carried the palanquin to the Forbidden City on their shoulders.

11 Guard of honour
Hundreds of guards line the wedding route, protecting and honouring the new empress.

GOLDEN PALANQUIN

Filled with pride in their important duty, the imperial envoys have set out to fetch Princess Jinfeng, the 21-year-old bride-to-be of China's emperor, Guangxu, and bring her to the heart of the Forbidden City. The carriage, or litter, they are carrying is known as the Phoenix Palanquin. Jinfeng will travel within it; her feet will not touch the ground until she reaches the Hall of Supreme Harmony, where the marriage will take place.

Empress Jinfeng
Jinfeng was a member of the powerful Yehe Nara clan of northeast China. Hers was an arranged marriage and the Guangxu Emperor was her cousin. Jinfeng was hand-picked for Guangxu by Cixi, the influential aunt of both empress and emperor.

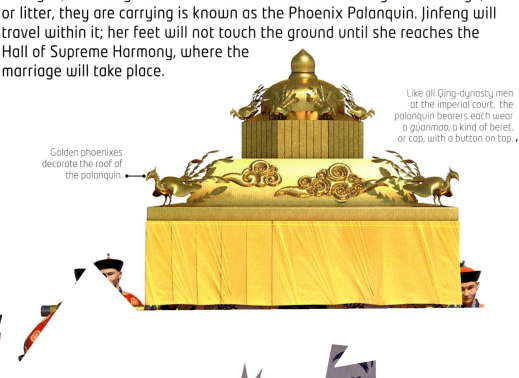

Like all Qing-dynasty men at the imperial court, the palanquin bearers each wear a *guanmao*, a kind of beret, or cap, with a button on top.

Golden phoenixes decorate the roof of the palanquin.

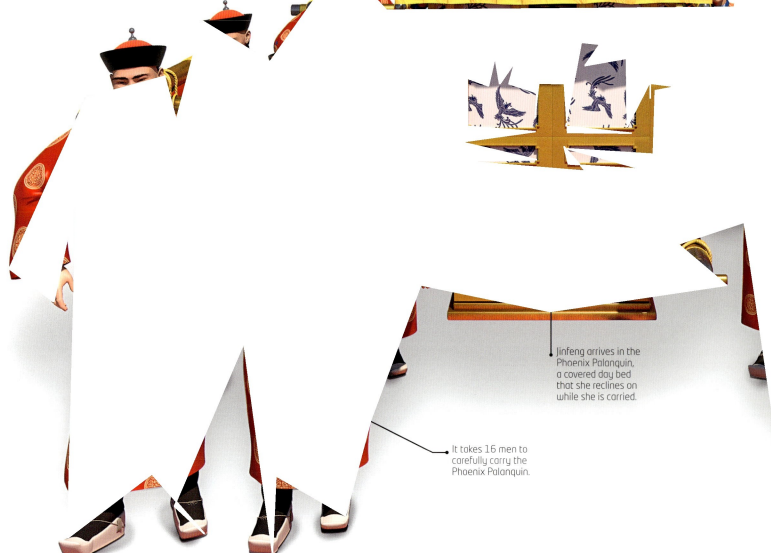

Jinfeng arrives in the Phoenix Palanquin, a covered day bed that she reclines on while she is carried.

It takes 16 men to carefully carry the Phoenix Palanquin.

Wedding gift

On their wedding day, Jinfeng and the emperor exchanged ceremonial sceptres known as *ruyi*. Originally backscratchers, gold, silver, and bejewelled *ruyi* became traditional royal wedding gifts.

Ceremonial gongs

Musicians announced the royal wedding by beating a *yunluo*, or "cloud gong". Its 10 bronze gongs varied in thickness, each one sounding a different tone when it was struck by a small mallet, or hammer.

Royal robes

The servants escorting Jinfeng on her wedding day were dressed in colourful patterned robes. They were finely embroidered in silk, and included scenes showing imperial dragons, as well as flowers, mountains, and seas that celebrated the beauty of China's landscape.

Special shoes

Lotus shoes were worn on important occasions. They would only fit someone whose feet had been bound. This was the painful practice where a woman's feet and toes were tightly bandaged to stop them growing.

Nail ornaments

Wealthy Chinese men and women wore their fingernails long to show that they did not have to do any manual labour. Jinfeng's long nails would have been covered by highly decorated nail guards for her wedding, to emphasize her power and prestige.

Fetching the bride

When it was time to collect Jinfeng for the wedding, a small group of men carried the Phoenix Palanquin to her residence, so she could be transported to the wedding hall in style.

CENTRE OF THE IMPERIAL UNIVERSE

The emperor is ready to receive his first guests of the day. He is dressed in his official Dragon Robe and seated on the Dragon Throne. In his eyes, and in those of all his people, he is the most powerful man alive. As proof, his throne is placed in the middle of the Hall of Supreme Harmony in the Forbidden City – the very spot the subjects of the empire believe to be the centre of the world.

A 3.4 m-high (11 ft) golden dragon sits at either end of the palace's roof, symbolizing imperial power.

No nails are used in the building at all. Everything is held together by strong interlocking wooden joints called *dougong*.

The pillars surrounding the throne are engraved with dragons, representing the heavenly dragons that pull the Sun across the sky each day in Chinese mythology.

Five dragons coil around the back and armrests of the throne.

Dragon Throne
Only the emperor could sit upon the golden Dragon Throne. It sat at the top of seven steps, to make sure the emperor was always raised high above those around him.

Approaching the emperor
Visitors to the emperor had to kowtow. This meant kneeling in front of him and knocking their head nine times on the floor. The louder the noise this made, the happier the emperor was.

The Hall of Supreme Ha[...] largest wooden building [...] It covers an area of 2,37[...] (25,586 sq ft), nearly the size [...] two Olympic swimming pools.

Pots buried in the floor amplify the noise when someone is kowtowing.

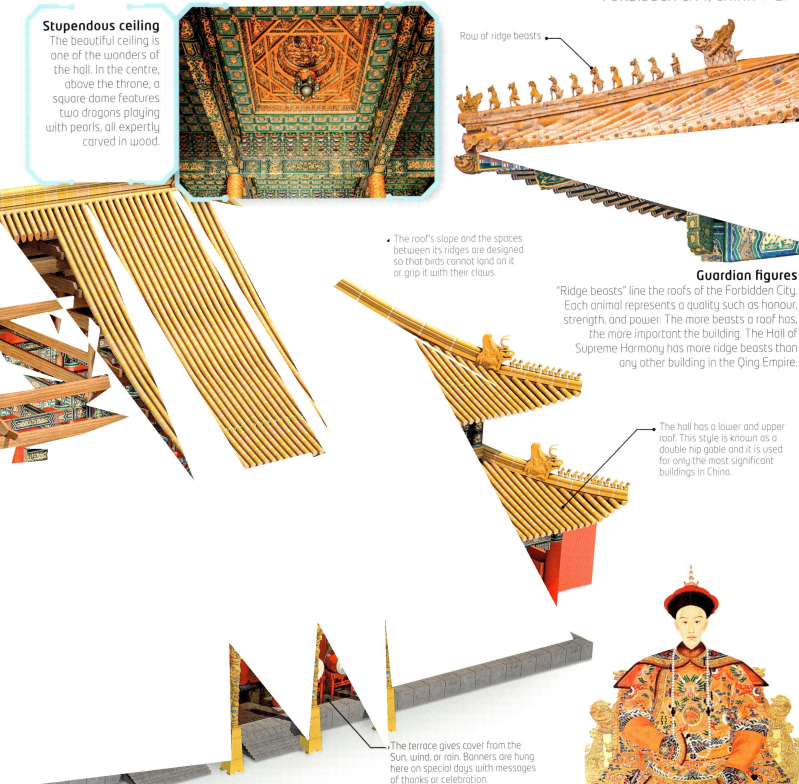

Stupendous ceiling
The beautiful ceiling is one of the wonders of the hall. In the centre, above the throne, a square dome features two dragons playing with pearls, all expertly carved in wood.

Row of ridge beasts

The roof's slope and the spaces between its ridges are designed so that birds cannot land on it or grip it with their claws.

Guardian figures
"Ridge beasts" line the roofs of the Forbidden City. Each animal represents a quality such as honour, strength, and power. The more beasts a roof has, the more important the building. The Hall of Supreme Harmony has more ridge beasts than any other building in the Qing Empire.

The hall has a lower and upper roof. This style is known as a double hip gable and it is used for only the most significant buildings in China.

The terrace gives cover from the Sun, wind, or rain. Banners are hung here on special days with messages of thanks or celebration.

Three visitors kowtow in front of the emperor on his Dragon Throne. They hope he will listen kindly to the messages they bring.

"I have often thought that I am the **most clever woman** that ever lived, and others **cannot compare with me**"
- Empress Dowager Cixi -

Guangxu Emperor
Guangxu became emperor in 1871, when he was just three years old, and his aunt, Cixi, ruled in his name. As he grew older, Guangxu attempted to modernize China. In 1898, he issued over 40 decrees that touched almost every aspect of society in a period known as the Hundred Days. But Cixi took back control and confined Guangxu to the Forbidden City where he was poisoned on 14 November 1908. His aunt is one of the suspects.

HALL OF MENTAL CULTIVATION

It is the mid-1880s, and the young Guangxu Emperor is receiving ambassadors from the northern borders in the Hall of Mental Cultivation. This is his private office, away from the more formal halls of the Forbidden City. While the emperor faces the ambassadors, his aunt and advisor, Cixi, hides behind a curtain and tells him what to say.

Emperor's chambers
The Hall of Mental Cultivation was originally the emperor's private office. Eventually, it came to replace the grander Hall of Supreme Harmony as the place where he received many of his guests.

Headgear holder

This colourful object is a hat stand. It is decorated with clouds and bats, and was used by the emperor to ensure his silk and fur hats kept their shape. It was extremely important for the emperor to look smart and dignified at all times.

The hollow stand is studded with holes so air can still circulate when a hat is on it.

Feng shui disc

China's emperors believed in feng shui, the idea that the position of furniture, pictures, and ornaments in a room can bring good or bad luck. This jade disc from the Hall of Mental Cultivation has a hole cut in it so that bad luck, ill health, and weakness could flow out of the building.

TREASURE BOX

In 2018, conservationists working on the roof of the Hall of Mental Cultivation found a hidden treasure box. Dating from around 1800, it contained coins bearing the words "May the world be peaceful", documents, metal ingots, incense, medicines, and other documents. Treasure boxes were often placed in the roofs of important buildings such as this to bring good luck.

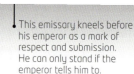

This emissary kneels before his emperor as a mark of respect and submission. He can only stand if the emperor tells him to.

The shadow formed by the marker on the sundial points to the current hour.

Sundial

Although mechanical clocks were available in China, there were still many sundials in the Forbidden City. This one stood outside the Hall of Mental Cultivation. If the emperor wanted to know the time, he could only find out if the sun was shining.

Delicate wooden carvings decorate the entrances to the back room where Cixi issues her orders.

Guangxu's aunt, Empress Dowager Cixi, whispers instructions to the boy emperor. As a woman at this time, she cannot be seen telling him what to do in public, however much she would like to.

Cixi's silk-covered chair was the closest she got to having a throne, even though she was a regent for two boy emperors during her lifetime.

Eastern Warmth Chamber

This room in the Hall of Mental Cultivation is named for the underfloor heating system that kept it warm in winter. Behind the emperor's throne is Cixi's chair, usually hidden by a curtain.

The young Guangxu Emperor listens to the report from the northern provinces. They are asking for more troops to protect the border.

A silk curtain hangs between the emperor and his aunt. The material is thick enough that Cixi cannot be seen, but thin enough for Guangxu to hear what she tells him.

CHARMED PHOENIX

Of all the ridge guardians on a Chinese building, the most important was the one at the tip of each corner of the roof. On the Hall of Supreme Harmony, this is a glazed figurine of the Heavenly Being, an immortal riding on a giant phoenix. It represents luck and good fortune.

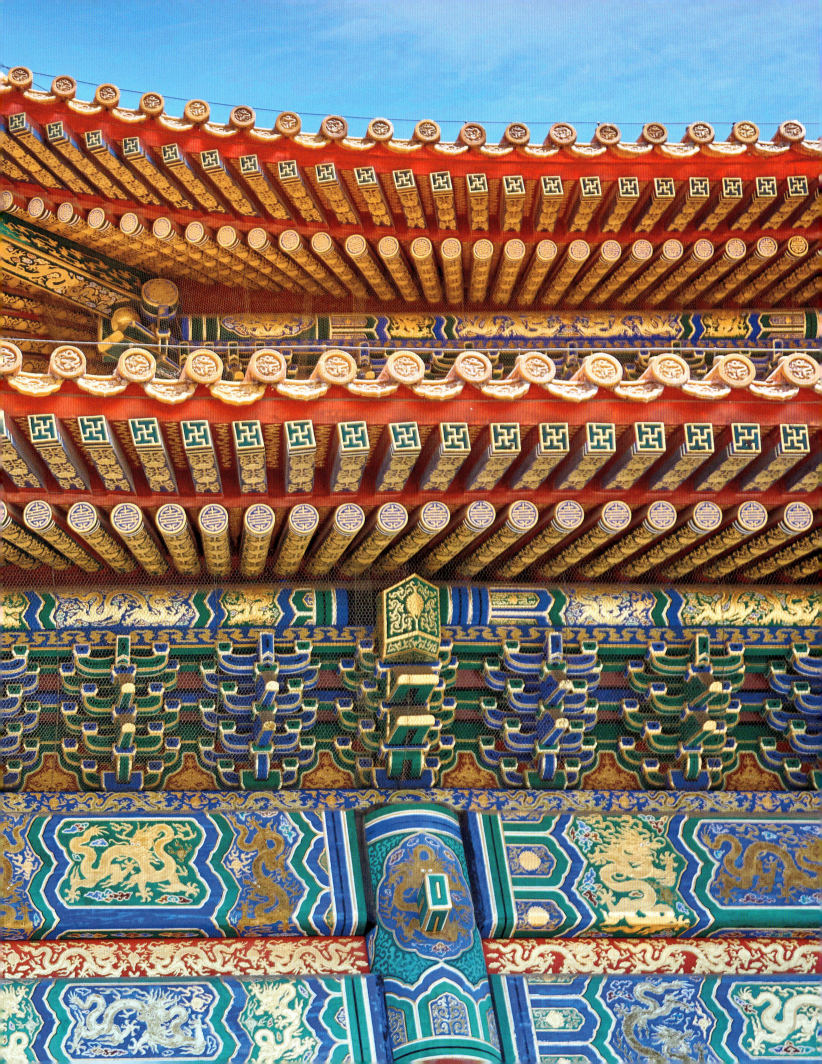

GLOSSARY

Ambassador
See Diplomat

Amulet
A small object believed to ward off evil spirits, illness, or danger.

Ancestor
A person who lived in the past, and who is a distant relative of people who are alive today.

Archaeologist
A person who excavates sites to reveal their history, by studying the objects and human remains found there.

Artefact
An object made by someone, such as a beautiful vase, or a useful pot or tool.

Artisan
A skilled craftsperson who produces things by hand.

BCE
A term meaning "Before the Common Era", placed after a date to indicate it happened before year 0, which is the start of the "Common Era", or CE.

Buddhism
A religion originating in India in the 6th–5th centuries BCE, based on the teachings of the Buddha. It spread throughout Asia and, later, the world.

Byzantine Empire
A powerful empire founded in 330 CE, centred around Constantinople (Istanbul). It dominated the Mediterranean region until conquered by the Ottoman Empire in 1453.

Canyon
A long narrow gorge through a rock, usually formed by a river eroding the rock over time.

Calligraphy
Handwriting produced as a highly valued art form, especially in Arabic, Chinese, Japanese, and Korean script.

Caravan
A train of animals or people, used to transport goods across long distances, especially along trade routes in Africa and Asia.

Cast
A copy of an original artefact, made by pouring plaster into a mould. In archaeology, plaster is poured into holes formed in the earth when bodies and artefacts buried there have decayed.

CE
Abbreviation for "Common Era", used in dates (*see* BCE).

Citizen
A person who belongs to a city or a bigger community, such a state or country, and has certain rights.

City-state
A city, and its surrounding territory, that has its own independent government.

Colonial
A term now used to describe the often negative and racist attitudes of people who have colonized lands outside their own country, expressed about that land or its people. In older texts, it usually just describes something relating to or created by the colonizers, such as "colonial architecture".

Colony
An area forced to be under the political and economic control of another state, usually in a foreign country.

Commercial
To do with trade and selling goods for a profit.

Compound
In architecture, a group of buildings arranged around a yard, often walled, where people live.

Confucianism
A religious philosophy originating in China, focusing on respect and learning.

Culture
The customs, beliefs, and behaviour shared by a society, or large group of people in that society.

Deity
A god or a goddess.

Diplomat
A person appointed by a country or other political body to carry out negotiations and maintain relationships with other countries. The highest rank of diplomat is ambassador.

Divine
Something that relates to a god or goddess, of any religion.

Dynasty
A family ruling a country for successive generations.

Emperor/Empress
The absolute ruler of an empire.

Empire
A group of lands or peoples under the rule of a single government or person.

Enslaved
Enslaved people are forced to work with no pay and have no rights. The system of owning people as property is known as slavery.

Excavate
In archaeology, to dig up an area in an organized way in order to find remains of buildings, people, and artefacts.

Excavation
An area being dug up for archaeological purposes.

Façade
The front section of a building, visible from the outside.

Fortress
See Fortification

Fortification
A strong building or set of buildings, designed to withstand attacks and protect the people inside it.

Fresco
Art painted directly on a wet plaster wall.

Frieze
A decorative carving running along the wall of a building.

Government
A group of people governing a country, often (but not always) elected to do so.

Iberian Peninsula
The region of Europe that is now Portugal and Spain.

Immigrant
A person leaving one nation to move to another country and settle there.

Import
The purchase of goods and services from other countries.

Ivory
The sought-after material taken from elephant tusks and used in artefacts (today illegally so).

Kingdom
A state or area ruled over by a king or queen.

Manuscript
A document written by hand, the common form of book before printing was invented.

Mausoleum
A large tomb built to contain the remains of a ruler or other important person.

Medieval
Describes anything dating from or taking place during the 6th to the 15th centuries, especially in Europe.

Merchant
A person who buys or sells goods.

Mesoamerica
A historical region with similar cultures that includes Mexico (in North America) and many of the countries in Central America.

Monolith
A large, tall stone that was raised to stand straight up.

Mosaic
A decoration made from small pieces of glass, stone, or tile stuck into position to make a picture or pattern.

Muslim
A follower of Islam, the religion founded in Mecca by the Prophet Muhammad in the 7th century.

Native American
A term for the indigenous peoples that first lived in North America – before the arrival of the Europeans – and still do.

Naval
Describing something to do with the navy, or ships in general.

Neolithic
The later Stone Age, during which improved stone weapons were made and the first farming began.

Noble
A member of the nobility or aristocracy, with more rights and privileges than people who were peasants or merchants.

Ottoman Empire
A large empire ruled by the Ottoman Turks from 1299 to 1923. It was at the height of its power in the 16th century.

Pavilion
A small building, often made to be decorative rather than just practical, and with a roof resting on pillars instead of walls.

Petroglyph
A carving or painting made on a rock.

Pharaoh
A title given to a king in ancient Egypt. People believed that pharaohs had sacred powers and were descended from the Sun god, Ra.

Philosophy
Thoughts about the deep questions of human existence, including what is right and wrong, true and false.

Pilgrim
A religious person who makes a journey to a holy place.

Pilgrimage
A religious journey to a holy place.

Relief
A sculpture only partly rising out from a flat background; often used to decorate vertical surfaces of monuments.

Renaissance
A period of European history, beginning in the 14th century, when art, architecture, and literature were influenced by the rediscovery of the ancient civilization around the Mediterranean.

Ritual
A set of actions with spiritual or religious meaning of any kind, performed in a particular way or order.

Sacred
Considered holy, and with religious significance, often related to a god or goddess.

Sanctuary
A holy or sacred place, such as a temple or church. Also a place where people could seek shelter and protection.

Sandstone
A naturally occurring type of sedimentary rock, often used as building material.

Scholar
A learned person, who studies and knows a lot about a subject.

Scribe
A person who wrote official documents and records, or copied manuscripts by hand, before printing was invented.

Script
The written characters that make up an alphabet.

Settlement
A place where people have settled down and built homes.

Shrine
A building or place considered sacred and usually dedicated to a god, spirit, or holy object.

Smelting
A process used to extract metals from rocks that contain them, known as ores.

Society
A group of people who live together or who are involved in a community together.

State
A country, or region within a country, which has its own government

Stupa
A mound-shaped structure for holding relics linked to the Buddha, often used as a shrine.

Sultan
Title of a ruler of some Muslim countries or regions, often historic, such as Al-Andalus (Andalucia) in what is now Spain.

Tablet
In ancient times, a flat piece of clay that people wrote on using a special tool called a stylus.

Temple
A building for religious worship or ceremonies.

Territory
A geographic area that has come under the control of a government.

Trade route
Established routes along which merchants, caravans, or ships loaded with goods travelled.

INDEX

Page numbers in **bold**
type refer to main entries

A

Acropolis, Greece 9, **48-49**
　Erechtheion Temple 56-57
　Great Panathenaia Procession
　　50-51
　Parthenon, Greece 6, 48-49,
　　52-53
　theatres **54-55**
Alexandria, Egypt 7
Alhambra Palace, Spain
　9, **108-109**, **110-111**,
　112-113
Amenhotep III, Pharaoh 26-27,
　28-29, **30-31**, 32-33
amphitheatres 54, 59
anthemion 52
antlers 15
arenas *see* Colosseum, Rome
Artemis, Temple of 6
astronomy 78, 82, 83, 107
Athena 48-49, 51, 52-53, 57

B

Babylonian Empire 7, 20-21,
　22-23, 25
ballgames 80-81
balls (dance parties) 134-135
Bantu people 114
baptism 92-93
battering rams 39, 40-41
Bedouin people 43
bedroom of Louis XIV
　138-139
birds 104, 114, 117
boats **51**
　Carthaginian 36-37, **38-39**
　Egyptian 28-29, 30-31
Borobudur, Indonesia 9, **96-97**,
　98-99, 100-101
Buddhism 73, 96-97, 98,
　100-101, 156
Byzantine Empire 86-87, 92,
　94-95, 156
　coronation ceremony 88-89,
　　90-91

C

calligraphy 129, 156
camels 42, 44
carriages 135, **136-137**, 148
Carthage Harbour, Tunisia
　9, **34-35**, **36-37**
　ships **38-39**, 40-41
castles 120-121, 122-123,
　124-125
　see also palaces
Chaco Canyon, USA 8, 102-103,
　104-105, 106-107
Chichen Itza, Mexico 8, **76-77**,
　84-85
　ballgame **80-81**
　observatory **82-83**
　Temple of Kukulcan **78-79**
China *see* Forbidden City, China
Christianity 86
churches 86-87, 90-91, 92
cities
　see also Chichen Itza, Mexico
　Carthage, Tunisia **34-35**,
　　36-37
　Great Zimbabwe 8, **114-115**,
　　116-117, 118-119
　Petra, Jordan 9, **42-43**,
　　44-45, 46-47
Cixi, Empress Dowager 148,
　151, 153
coins 36, 42, 53, 91, 117, 138
Colosseum, Rome 9, **58-59**,
　66-67, 68-69
　gladiator combat **60-61**,
　　62-63
　spectators **64-65**
Colossus of Rhodes 7
columns 48, 52, 76, 84-85, 110
Confucianism 126, 156
Constantine IV, Byzantine
　Emperor 89, 90-91
Constantinople, Turkey 49, 86,
　90, 95
cows 116, 117
crocodiles 70
cuneiform script 21, 23

D

diamonds 136
Dionysus 55
dogs 105

Dosan Seowon, South Korea
　9, **126-127**, **128-129**, 130
dragons 147, 150
Drepana, Battle of 39
Durrington Walls, England 11,
　16-17

E

Ecnomus, Battle of 36
Egypt 7, 30-31, 32, 43
　Malqata 26-27, 28-29
　elephants 98
England, UK **16-17**
　see also Stonehenge, England
equinoxes 11, 82, 103
Erechtheion Temple, Greece
　49, 56-57

F

Fajada Butte, USA 102, 103
feng shui 152
fireworks 141
Forbidden City, China
　9, **144-145**
　Hall of Mental Cultivation
　　152-153
　Hall of Supreme Harmony
　　150-151, 154-155
　wedding ceremony **146-147**,
　　148-149
France 122, **136-137**
　see also Versailles, France
frankincense 44

G

gardens
　Heidelberg Castle, Germany
　　121, 124-125
　Sigiriya, Sri Lanka 72, 73,
　　74-75
　Versailles, France 132,
　　140-141
Gate of Ishtar, Iraq 20-21,
　22-23, 24-25
Germany 120-121, 122-123,
　124-125
Giza, Great Pyramid of 7
gladiators 58-59, 61-62,
　62-63, 64, 66
glyphs 83, 106-107

gold 17, 115
graffiti 65
Granada, Kingdom of 108-109
great houses 102
Great Pyramid of Giza 7
Great Zimbabwe 8, **114-115**,
　116-117, 118-119
Greece 6-7, 62
　see also Acropolis, Greece
Guangxu Emperor 146,
　148-149, 151, 152-153
gunpowder 121, 122

H

Hadrian, Emperor 60, 61
Hagia Sophia, Turkey 9, **86-87**,
　94-95
　baptistry **92-93**
　coronation ceremony **88-89**,
　　90-91
Halicarnassus, Greece 6
Hall of Mental Cultivation
　152-153
Hall of Supreme Harmony
　150-151, 154-155
Hanging Gardens of Babylon
　7, 20
Hannibal 34, 36
harbours 34-35, 36-37
Heel Stone 10
Heidelberg Castle, Germany
　9, **120-121**, **122-123**,
　124-125
horses 137
huts 16-17
hypogeum 66-67

I

Ibn Zamrak 110
icons 92
incense 44, 145
Indonesia 9, 96-97, 98-99,
　100-101
Ishtar Gate, Iraq 9, **20-21**,
　22-23, 24-25

JK

Java 9, 96-97, 98-99, 100-101
Jinfeng, Empress 146-147,
　148-149

Jordan 9, 42-43, 44-45, 46-47
Joseon Dynasty 126
Justinian I, Byzantine Emperor 86, 87
Justinian II, Byzantine Emperor 89, 90-91
Kashyapa, King 70-71, 72-73
Korea, South 9, 126-127, 128-129, 130
kowtowing 150

L

Lighthouse of Alexandria 7
lions 21, 24, 71, 98, 147
Lions, Palace of the 109, 110-111, 112-113
Louis XIV, King of France 132-133, 136
   at Versailles 135, 138-139, 140-141, 142-143

M

Malqata, Egypt 9, 26-27, 28-29, 32
map, Babylonian 21
masks 34, 54, 130-131
Mausoleum at Halicarnassus 6
Maya civilization 76-77, 78-79, 80-81, 82-83
Meridian Gate 145
Mexico see Chichen Itza, Mexico
monoliths
   see Stonehenge, England
mosaics 34, 86, 92
mosques 48, 87
Muhammad I, Sultan of Granada 108
Muhammad V, Sultan of Granada 109, 111
muqarnas 111, 112

N

Nabatean people 42, 44
Native American civilization 8, 102-103, 104-105, 106-107
Nebuchadnezzar II 7, 21

O

observatories 82-83
Ottoman Empire 48, 87, 92, 95, 157

P

Palace of the Lions, Alhambra 109, 110-111, 112-113
palaces
   see also Forbidden City, China; Versailles, France
   Alhambra Palace, Spain 108-109, 110-111, 112-113
   Babylon 20
   Heidelberg Castle, Germany 120-121, 122-123, 124-125
   Malqata, Egypt 26-27, 28-29, 32
   Sigiriya, Sri Lanka 9, 70-71, 72-73, 74-75
palanquins 147, 148-149
Palantinate 122
Panathenaia Procession 50-51, 52
Parthenon, Greece 6, 48-49, 52-53
Pericles 48
Petra, Jordan 9, 42-43, 44-45, 46-47
petroglyphs 103, 106-107
Phidias 6, 53
Phoenician civilization 34, 38
Phoenix Palanquin 148-149
pilgrimages 98-99
ports 34-35, 36-37
prehistoric life 16-17
Pueblo Bonito, USA 8, 102-103, 104-105, 106-107
Punic Empire 34, 35, 39, 41
pyramids 7, 76, 79, 96

QR

Qing dynasty 144, 148, 151
quinqueremes 36, 38-39
rats 102
Ravana, King 70
Rhodes, Greece 7

Roman Empire 34-35, 36, 86
   see also Colosseum, Rome
   ships 38, 40-41
roses 90

S

scholars 128, 130
sedan chairs 141
Seonjo of Joseon, King of Korea 126
Seven Wonders of the Ancient World 6-7
shells 117
ships see boats
Sigiriya, Sri Lanka 9, 70-71, 72-73, 74-75
silks 91, 111, 149
snakes 76
soapstone artefacts 114, 117, 119
solar eclipse 78-79
solstices 10-11, 12-13, 103
South Korea 126-127, 128-129, 130-131
Spain 108-109, 110-111, 112-113
sports
   gladiators 58-59, 61-62, 62-63, 64, 66
   Maya ballgame 80-81
Sri Lanka 9, 70-71, 72-73, 74-75
stables 137
stadiums 80-81
   see also Colosseum, Rome
stage, theatre 54-55
Statue of Zeus 6
Stonehenge, England, UK 8, 10-11, 16, 18-19
   construction 14-15
   winter solstice ceremony 12-13
summer solstice 10-11, 103
sundials 153
Sun King 132, 143

T

teachers 126, 128
temples 6, 31, 34
   see also Acropolis, Greece
   Babylonian 22, 23

Roman Empire 34-35, 36, 86
   see also Colosseum, Rome
ships 38, 40-41
roses 90

Borobudur, Indonesia 9, 96-97, 98-99, 100-101
Maya 76-77, 78-79
theatres 54-55
tiles 112
Tiye, Queen consort of Egypt 28, 31, 32-33
toilets 65
tools 15
Topkapi Palace, Istanbul 94-95
Tunisia 34-35, 36-37
Turkey 6, 48, 66
   see also Hagia Sophia, Turkey

UV

United States of America 8, 102-103, 104-105, 106-107
Versailles, France 9, 132-133, 142-143
   balls 134-135
   King's bedroom 138-139
   gardens 137, 140-141
Vespasian, Emperor of Rome 58
villages 16-17, 102
volcanoes 70, 96

W

Wales, UK 15
Warriors, Temple of 77, 79, 85
wedding ceremonies 146-147, 148-149, 150-151
wigs 133
wine 121
winter solstice 11, 12-13
woodblock printing 129
writing 21, 23, 83, 129

YZ

Yi Hwang 126-127
Yongle Emperor of China 144, 145
Zeus, Statue of 6
Zimbabwe 8, 114-115, 116-117, 118-119

ACKNOWLEDGMENTS

DK would like to thank:
Elizabeth Wise for the index; Danielle Cluer Gee for proofreading; Simon Mumford for the maps; Ed Pearce for editorial help; Kit Lane for design help; Rob Perry for visualization; Katy Jakeway for additional illustrations.

The publisher would also like to thank the following for their kind permission to reproduce their photographs:

(Key: a-above; b-below/bottom; c-centre; f-far; l-left; r-right; t-top)

6 Alamy Stock Photo: Lebrecht Music & Arts (b); Pictures Now (t). **7 Bridgeman Images:** © Look and Learn (tl, bl). **8 akg-images:** De Agostini / G. Cappelli (cl). **Alamy Stock Photo:** Sergi Reboredo (bl); Christopher Scott (br). **Dreamstime. com:** Whpics (tr). **9 Alamy Stock Photo:** Aflo Co. Ltd. (tr); Calin Stan (tl); Jan Wlodarczyk (bl); Hemis (br). **Jord Hammond Photography:** (c). **10 Historic England Archive:** Courtesy of The Salisbury Museum (bl). **Mary Evans Picture Library:** Historic England (c). **10-11 Alamy Stock Photo:** Skyscan Photolibrary (c); Mark Stevens (bc). **15 Alamy Stock Photo:** Joan Gravell (cr). **Getty Images:** Matt Cardy (b). **Historic England Archive:** Courtesy of The Salisbury Museum (cla); Courtesy of The Salisbury Museum. (clb). **16 Alamy Stock Photo:** AA World Travel Library (tl). **Bridgeman Images:** Salisbury Museum (bc). **Dr Lisa-Marie Shillito:** (bl). **17 Alamy Stock Photo:** Neil Lang (br). **Dorling Kindersley:** Geoff Dann / Cotswold Farm Park, Gloucestershire (tr). **18-19 Alamy Stock Photo:** All Canada Photos. **20-21 Getty Images:** Hussein Faleh. **21 Alamy Stock Photo:** Prisma by Dukas Presseagentur GmbH (c); Ivan Vdovin (tl); World History Archive (tr); Science History Images (br). **23 Alamy Stock Photo:** Classic Image (tr); The Print Collector (bc). © **The Trustees of the British Museum. All rights reserved. 24-25 Alamy Stock Photo:** Peter Horree. **26 Alamy Stock Photo:** Album (c); MET / BOT (cra); PRISMA ARCHIVO (bl); Artokoloro (br). **Bridgeman Images:** NPL - DeA Picture Library / S. Vannini (cla). **26-27 Alamy Stock Photo:** Magica (t). **27 Alamy Stock Photo:** MET / BOT (bl). **Photo Scala, Florence:** Catharine H. Roehrig. © 2022 / The Metropolitan Museum of Art / Art Resource, NY (t). **30 akg-images:** 4294245 (bl). **Alamy Stock Photo:** Alain Guilleux (cl); The Picture Art Collection (tr). **31 Alamy Stock Photo:** Greg Balfour Evans (b); Magica (tl). **32-33 Alamy Stock Photo:** Ian M Butterfield. **34 Alamy Stock Photo:** Peter Horree (br); SJ Images (cl); Lucas Vallecillos (bl). **Bridgeman Images:** G. Dagli Orti / © NPL - DeA Picture Library (cr). **34-35 Getty Images:** Maremagnum (cr). **35 Alamy**

Stock Photo: Peter Horree (bl); Massimo Salesi (br). **36 Alamy Stock Photo:** agefotostock (tl); Heritage Image Partnership Ltd (cl); Peter Horree (bl, br). **38 Alamy Stock Photo:** Heritage Image Partnership Ltd (bl). **39 Alamy Stock Photo:** Peter Horree (br). **Getty Images:** DEA / ICAS94 (tr). **RPM Nautical Foundation:** Soprintendenza del Mare-Sicila (tl). **40-41 RPM Nautical Foundation:** Soprintendenza del Mare-Sicila. **42 Alamy Stock Photo:** Album (cl); Heritage Image Partnership Ltd (cr); CPA Media Pte Ltd (bl); Alexey Stiop (br). **43 Alamy Stock Photo:** Jan Wlodarczyk; World History Archive (br). **46-47 Alamy Stock Photo:** Ievgen Skrypko. **48 Alamy Stock Photo:** Gibon Art (cr); Peter Horree (c); INTERFOTO (clb); WorldFoto (b). **49 Alamy Stock Photo:** Aitan (bl); James Davis Photography (br). **Dorling Kindersley:** 123RF.com: Stefanos Kyriazis / thegreekphotoholic (t). **52 Alamy Stock Photo:** Album (cl); Mauritius Images GmbH / Marco Simoni (bl). **53 Alamy Stock Photo:** Chronicle (tr); INTERFOTO (tc); domonabikeUSA (br). **Dorling Kindersley:** Gary Ombler / University of Aberdeen (bl, bc). **54 Alamy Stock Photo:** Hercules Milas (cl); Santi Rodriguez (t); Gina Rodgers (bl); The Print Collector (br). **55 Alamy Stock Photo:** Album (tr); GRANGER - Historical Picture Archive (tc); Chronicle (b). **56-57 Shutterstock.com:** Lucky-photographer. **58 Alamy Stock Photo:** PRISMA ARCHIVO (cl, br); Calin Stan (bl). **58-59 Alamy Stock Photo:** Calin Stan. **59 Alamy Stock Photo:** Florilegius (br). **62 Alamy Stock Photo:** Artokoloro (bl); Endless Travel (cl). **63 Alamy Stock Photo:** Artokoloro (br); Lanmas (tl, tr); INTERFOTO (tc); PRISMA ARCHIVO (cl); Heritage Image Partnership Ltd (bl). **64 akg-images:** Peter Connolly (cl). **Alamy Stock Photo:** Steven Gillis hd9 imaging (bl). **65 Alamy Stock Photo:** Ancient Art and Architecture (br); Marshall Ikonography (tl); Azoor Photo (cr). **TopFoto:** Alinari (tr). **66 Alamy Stock Photo:** Abaca Press (bl). **Bridgeman Images:** Alinari (tl). **Dorling Kindersley:** Fotolia / Ivan Kmit (cl). **67 Alamy Stock Photo:** Rubens Alarcon (br). **68-69 Alamy Stock Photo:** Calin Stan. **70 Alamy Stock Photo:** Mauritius Images GmbH (br); Papilio (c). **Getty Images:** Avel Shah / EyeEm (cl). **71 Alamy Stock Photo:** imageBROKER (br). **Jord Hammond Photography.** **73 Alamy Stock Photo:** AlamyTim82 (br). **Bridgeman Images:** Pictures from History (tr). **Getty Images:** Wolfgang Kaehler (tl); Tuul & Bruno Morandi (bl). **74-75 Getty Images:** Frans Sellies. **76 Alamy Stock Photo:** Diego Grandi (cl); J.Enrique Molina (bl). **Dorling Kindersley:** Dreamstime.com / Lunamarina (br). **76-77 Alamy Stock Photo:** Sergi Reboredo (tr). **77 Alamy Stock Photo:** GRANGER - Historical Picture Archive (br). **Dorling Kindersley:** (bc). **80 Alamy Stock Photo:** Russell Mills Travel

(t). **81 Alamy Stock Photo:** Cavan Images (br); GRANGER - Historical Picture Archive (cr). **Los Angeles County Museum of Art:** The Proctor Stafford Collection, purchased with funds provided by Mr. and Mrs. Allan C. Balch (t). **82 Alamy Stock Photo:** Science History Images (tl). **83 Alamy Stock Photo:** Sébastien Lecocq (br); PNC Collection (tc); World History Archive (bc). **Los Angeles County Museum of Art:** Purchased with funds provided by Camilla Chandler Frost (M.2010.115.628) (tr). **84-85 Shutterstock.com:** Subbotina Anna. **86 Alamy Stock Photo:** Heritage Image Partnership Ltd (bc). **Bridgeman Images:** © AISA (br); Granger (cr). **Dorling Kindersley:** (cl). **86-87 Alamy Stock Photo:** Roland Nagy (tr). **87 Dorling Kindersley:** (br). **90 Alamy Stock Photo:** Heritage Image Partnership Ltd (tl). **Bridgeman Images:** Grace Rainey Rogers Fund (bc). **91 Alamy Stock Photo:** Album (bc); CelCinar (tr); Peregrine (cr). **92 Alamy Stock Photo:** Artokoloro (cr); David Pearson (bl); GRANGER - Historical Picture Archive (br). **Bridgeman Images. Getty Images / iStock:** minemero (tr). **94-95 Getty Images:** Anadolu Agency. **96 Alamy Stock Photo:** Danvis Collection (b); FOST (c). **Shutterstock.com:** Assabili / EPA (br). **96-97 Alamy Stock Photo:** Hemis (tr). **97 Alamy Stock Photo:** Artokoloro (bl); Jane Sweeney (br). **98 Alamy Stock Photo:** agefotostock (cl); Gnomeandi (cr); Sabena Jane Blackbird (bl). **Getty Images:** John Elk III (c). **100-101 Alamy Stock Photo:** Jorge Fernandez. **102 Alamy Stock Photo:** Rick & Nora Bowers (cr); Thomas Levine Photography (cla); Design Pics Inc (clb); Buddy Mays (b). **102-103 akg-images:** De Agostini / G. Cappelli (t). **103 Alamy Stock Photo:** Efrain Padro (bl). **104 Alamy Stock Photo:** PB / YB (cl). **Getty Images:** Ger Bosma (cr); Werner Forman (bl). **106-107 Getty Images:** Daniel A. Leifheit. **108-109 Alamy Stock Photo:** Kavalenkava Volha (b). **109 Alamy Stock Photo:** Album (cr); Matt MacMurchy (tl); Heritage Image Partnership Ltd (tr); Ian Dagnall (cl); imageBROKER (bl). **111 Alamy Stock Photo:** Historic Images (b); Kumar Sriskandan (tc); MAEKFOTO (c). **Dreamstime.com:** Mangojuicy (r). **112-113 Alamy Stock Photo:** funkyfood London / Paul Williams. **114 Alamy Stock Photo:** Universal Images Group North America LLC / DeAgostini (br). © **The Trustees of the British Museum. All rights reserved:** (c). **Getty Images:** Denny Allen (bl). **Shutterstock.com:** Stuart Forster (br). **114-115 Alamy Stock Photo:** Christopher Scott (t). **115 Alamy Stock Photo:** Christopher Scott (br). **Getty Images:** Heritage Images (bl). **117 Professor Shadreck Chirikure:** (t). **Getty Images:** DE AGOSTINI PICTURE LIBRARY (cr); Werner Forman / Universal Images Group (b). **118-119 Alamy Stock Photo:** Christopher Scott. **120-121 Alamy**

Stock Photo: Hans Blossey (b). **121 Alamy Stock Photo:** DP Landscapes (tl, tr); imageBROKER (cl); Jochen Tack (cr); Prisma by Dukas Presseagentur GmbH (b). **122 Alamy Stock Photo:** Heritage Image Partnership Ltd (tl). **Bridgeman Images:** Stefano Bianchetti (bl). **Dreamstime. com:** Andrew Baumert (br). **Library of Congress, Washington, D.C.:** (tr). **124-125 Getty Images:** DEA / Albert Ceolan. **126 Alamy Stock Photo:** Korean Painting (bl); Matteo Omied (cl); Ivan Vdovin (cr); REUTERS (br). **126-127 Alamy Stock Photo:** Aflo Co. Ltd. (t). **127 Alamy Stock Photo:** Dirk Renckhoff (br). **129 Alamy Stock Photo:** National Museum of Korea: (tl). **130-131 Shutterstock. com:** Kobby Dagan. **132 Alamy Stock Photo:** Zip Lexing (bl); Pictures Now (c). **Bridgeman Images:** Wallace Collection, London (br). **132-133 Alamy Stock Photo:** Barbara Ash (t). **133 Alamy Stock Photo:** GALA Images ARCHIVE (br). **Bridgeman Images:** Heritage Image Partnership Ltd (cl); REUTERS (bl). **137 Alamy Stock Photo:** MET / BOT (br); The Picture Art Collection (bl). **Bridgeman Images. 138 Alamy Stock Photo:** Heritage Image Partnership Ltd (t); MET / BOT (c). **Photo Scala, Florence:** Christophe Fouin / © 2022. RMN-Grand Palais / Dist (b). **139 akg-images:** CDA / Guillemot (tr); Liszt Collection (cr); Les Arts Décoratifs. Paris / Jean Tholance (br). **140 Bridgeman Images. Photo Scala, Florence:** Musée de l'Armée © 2022 / RMN-Grand Palais / Dist (bl). **141 Bridgeman Images:** Archives Charmet (br). **Photo Scala, Florence:** Jean-Marc Manai © 2022 / RMN-Grand Palais (tr). **142-143 Bridgeman Images:** Luca Tettoni. **144-145 Alamy Stock Photo:** Sean Pavone (b). **145 Alamy Stock Photo:** incamerastock (br); Paul Springett D (t). **Bridgeman Images:** Pictures from History / David Henley (bl). **Getty Images:** Sino images (c). **148 Alamy Stock Photo:** The Picture Art Collection (tl). **149 Alamy Stock Photo:** Album (tr); Eraza Collection (tl); MET / BOT (cla); Heritage Image Partnership Ltd (cra); VTR (br). **TopFoto:** Pictures From History (c). **150 akg-images:** Mel Longhurst (cl). **Alamy Stock Photo. 151 Alamy Stock Photo:** CPA Media Pte Ltd (br); TAO Images Limited (tc); DV TRAVEL (tr). **152 Alamy Stock Photo:** Carol Barrington (tr); Imaginechina Limited (b). **Dreamstime. com:** Jeffrey Chia (cr). **Getty Images:** South China Morning Post (cl). **153 Alamy Stock Photo:** TAO Images Limited (t); TAO Images Limited (b). **154-155 Alamy Stock Photo:** Jan Wlodarczyk.

All other images © Dorling Kindersley